Trust in Yourself

Messages from the Divine

Jaya Sarada

With deep gratitude to Joni Takanikos
for long hours of editing

and Laura Stevens who assisted in the process

Heart Chakra Mandala graphic Karen Foster Wells

Cover Design: Abigail Thompson
Book Design: Linne Ha
Lotus Photography: Arielle Clarke in Bali 1997

Printed by Book Crafters 734-475-9145
Published by Grace Publishing 1-800-282-5292
Author may be contacted through Grace Foundation
PO Box 1081 Freeland WA 98249 USA
Tel: 360-331-5360

Library of Congress: 98-93634
ISBN: 1-893037-00-2

That which permeates all,
which nothing transcends and which,
like the universal space around us,
fills everything completely from within and without,
that Supreme non-dual Brahman—that thou art.

SANKARACHARYA

The Gayatri Mantra

Aum; Bhoor Bhuvah Sva-ha
(Om, O Thou Who givest sustenance to the Universe)

Tat Svitar Var e'-unyum
From whom all things proceed

Dhiyo-Yo Nahf Pracho-dayaat.
And to Whom all things return

Unveil to us the face of the true Spiritual Sun,
Hidden by a disc of golden light
That we my know the truth,
And do our whole duty
As we journey to Thy Sacred Feet

CONTENTS

Dedicated to my Soul Family:
My dearest divine Mother, her life is an example of
living truth and divine love.
My beloved sister, Sandhya, who lives her life in direct contact
with the divine.
My dearest brother, Brad, who is a walking sage that moves
through life with complete knowing. Shawna, his partner and my
soul sister, who touches this earth with her angelic wings.
Thomas, my eternal friend and partner in life,
who is one with the ocean of life.
My precious daughter, Arielle, who dances
to the tune of God's melody.
My loving daughter, Alyssa, a pillar of strength and wisdom.
My Father and Grandmother, now in Spirit,
who guided me to Grace.
My sacred circle of friends, who share with me
the very flame that makes us one.

INTRODUCTION

NAMASTE! I SALUTE THE DIVINITY WITHIN YOU!

The spark of divinity is within you, the very root of your being, your one and only reality is that you are a fragment of the life of God. In essence, you are the highest aspect of yourself, the inner-most source of your being, the well-spring of life. Your soul has been veiled in the temporary garment of the physical, emotional and mental bodies, but you are completely free from this condition. Your divine nature far transcends the limitations of thoughts and emotions. The divine spark within you moves through all limitations of your physical conditions, into divine manifestation.

Your true essence is eternal and untouched by disease and disharmony. The consciousness of your soul is devoted to divine essence in reality, whereas the identification of the lower mind and emotions focuses on the details of the physical plane. Thoughts that are generated from the principles of pure consciousness have a powerful effect on your life.

Meditation and concentration on the eternal plane raise your consciousness to the state of knowing your true reality. Intuition evolves to assist you to see from the inside and discern that "which is" from outer sources. Pure love and reason, the nature of true knowledge become congruous with the pure self.

When the pure self transcends the lower nature of the personality, the higher aspect of pure consciousness takes control, expressing from the point of self-lessness rather than selfishness. Working in harmony with the Divine is the work of the pure self, creating a deep and lasting goodness. All experiences in your life are passed through the sieve of the true self, a filter of awakening light.

The personality when unified with its higher nature is now in the divine order of the sacred within. In discovering that which is eternal or ever-present, the pure consciousness of your being, the unreal falls away. The temporary aspects of your makeup, the physical, emotional and mental natures are seen as just passing scenes in the drama of life. It is when awareness moves beyond the limitation of this physical plane, that you touch into the deep inner core, your real essence.

The journey into the pure light of your being brings joy, beauty, understanding and a sense of wholeness and well being. In each human being there are certain spiritual tests or illusionary walls to break through. The emotional body brings the test of desire, and a great pull to fulfill desires that display in your consciousness. In Sanskrit this is called *Kama,* that means the combination of feeling and sensation. It is the personal self that is identified with the state of temporary desires and the seeking to fulfill them. We often think of these desires as our very essence and fail to discriminate between that which is passing and our true self, which does not change upon the satisfaction of desire.

There is another saying in Sanskrit called "Amkara," *Aham* meaning "I" and *Kara* meaning "making," thus translates as "I-maker." This refers to the endless cycle of living to satisfy the "I" consciousness, in pursuit of filling up the emptiness of the personal self. It is through the giving away to these desires we become bound to the endless cycle of birth and death.

Manas is the Sanskrit word for mind, completing the concept of the most powerful web we find ourselves in "The Kama-Manasic state." This state is when the mind is mixed with emotions, the most difficult state to overcome in the realization of the pure self within.

When emotions are mastered and thought is no longer followed out in pursuit of self-gain, your pure essence of love can be turned toward the ever-abiding happiness and peace of your true nature. It is through the act of turning inward, that the heart begins the process of healing, for the love of the divine is the love of your true essence.

The mechanism of the mind is two fold, the lower aspect in Sanskrit is called *rupa*, meaning "having form" and the higher aspect of the mind is called *arupa* or "without form." The lower part of the mind is identified with the temporary personality, which creates a strong obstacle in the realization of your true self.

The term *Asmita,* in Sanskrit meaning "I am this," is the condition of being that is strongly identified with the physical plane, convinced that *this* is the only reality. As long as you identify with the ego-self, or personality, you block the light of the soul. Serving the personality for self interests, you create a great bondage to earth pleasure and seeds for future incarnations.

Thoughts tainted with emotions are very difficult because of the powerful illusionary nature of this combination. The lower mind, or the objective mind, is conditioned by the external appearances of life. Because this aspect of our intelligence deals with concrete information; life actions are based on limited knowledge from physical manifestation.

As you loosen your grip on worldly identification, you will develop the insight and perception to see the essence of life. The *ajna,* or third eye develops, creating an inner vision. Action on the physical plane then arises from an inward impression of the higher world and intuition. The higher mental body when developed can inspire the essence of your true nature, illuminating the light of your being.

The path to your true nature brings many tests and obstacles. This is life's way of purifying and releasing all aspects of your personal self. Relaxing into your true essence, life's tests become divine grace, lighting that path home.

In our deep conditioning we think this world, and all that is in it, is reality. This reality requires serious investigation, going inward in silence to observe the part of us that is pure being and pure consciousness. When perception of your true reality occurs, you can just relax, let go of all identification with what is temporary. The interplay with mind and emotions create a stormy life for the individual.

The habitual nature of thought and the sensation of pleasure is to store it in our memory and go through life trying to repeat it. We often spend our life in the turbulence of emotions, passions, and desires, seeking that which is pleasurable and running away from that which is painful.

This struggle is a long and arduous process as the sum total of the personality is deeply embedded in identification with itself. The true self has the task of mastering the personality, in the process of becoming a whole human being. This becomes a spiritual battle that can go on for many lifetimes, until there is a complete recognition of your true eternal nature.

The meeting place of your true self is when you live in the heart of silence where the light of wisdom and love reside. Your true essence, a divine eternal spark is whole and untouched by all disease and disharmony. It is through quiet contemplation of your inner true reality that the journey deepens into the core of the heart where the veil of illusion falls away. This sacred journey is the return to what is always present, residing in the heart and illuminating your path home.

"Trust in Yourself" for there is no other reality but your true ever-abiding self. Delving deeper and deeper within, you will feel the oneness of all creation and live in the pure consciousness of being. It will become apparent that you are the same pure consciousness that is within all beings. The only difference between you and the next person is that you have decided to take the leap out of suffering to live in the realm of true self knowledge and awareness.

Follow your inner conscience for that is the voice of your true self. Deep inside beyond all conditions of your personality is a being of goodness and holiness; it is only through strong identification with the ego-self, of the ego that you have lost touch with your truth. Turn within to your ever-abiding source of infinite love and wisdom. To begin, **"Trust in Yourself!"**

This work is dedicated to the living flame that resides in all hearts;
throughout all changes this flame burns in one's eternal nature,
guiding, protecting and nurturing, we are one as the flame is one.
Attending to the flame illuminates our journey home.

The seeker is he who is in search of himself

Give up all questions except one: Who am I?' After all, the only

fact you are sure of is that you are. The 'I am' is certain.

The 'I am this' is not. Struggle to find out what you are in reality.

To know what you are, you must first investigate

what you are not.

Discover all that you are not—body, feelings, thoughts, time,

space, this or that. The end of the search is when you come to this

understanding and you realize that you are the limitless being.

SRI NISARGADATTA MAHARAJ

CHAPTER ONE

TRUST IN THE LIGHT THAT YOU ARE

Be a Light unto Yourself
The Essential Question
Beyond Thoughts, Emotions and Conditioning
Trust in the Light that You Are
Meditation: The Light of the Spiritual Heart

BE A LIGHT UNTO YOURSELF

There is an ever-abiding light within you waiting in stillness. This is the light of your true nature, the sacred essence within you. You are destined for a great encounter with your true reality. This reality which is before thought, before sensation and before identification with anything, is your true self, pure and simple.

Your true nature is pure consciousness, witnessing the appearing and disappearing of thoughts and emotions. The personal self is founded in mistaken identification, taking itself to be a separate reality, identifying with thoughts and emotions for the purpose of self-gratification. This self-gratifying activity of the personal self becomes a deep pattern of suffering throughout many human lives. The ego is created by this separate sense of self, engaging and following thought out for the purpose of self-gain, creating a web of desire. The 'I' thought, is the very nature of separation, creating an illusionary self that seeks to be maintained. Your true reality then becomes veiled in the false identification of who you think you are, a separate individual, striving to maintain its separate identity.

When the ego, the separate individual, returns to the light of pure consciousness, there is complete peace and wholeness of being. When you live the light you are, you remain in constant recognition of your true nature in daily life. Your reality is that you are a pure being, unbounded by all external influences. All worldly accumulation is subject to time and death, as is this temporary body. What resides within you is an ever-lasting, infinite spiritual being. This realization is the fuel for self inquiry, leading you to go within, and meet the eternal self that resides in your spiritual heart.

Your true nature is eternal consciousness, which is not subject to birth or death, holding nothing, and is in essence pure emptiness. Your true essence is a pure and continual consciousness that moves in and out of experiences for the purpose of self-realization. In your true reality, you remain untouched by all experiences, while remaining deeply connected to the everlasting sacredness of life. We are sacred beings traveling in these temporary bodies, but untouched by the conditions of this birth.

The personal self is subject to the conditions of thoughts and emotions because of habits and patterns embedded through the false identification of the self. Identification with the ego, with its roots in separation, will maintain its stance of importance as long as your attention is outward bound. When your attention is turned inward to the source of your being, you will discover your true sacred nature. This inward looking will light the path of inquiry as you embark upon your essential nature.

As you begin to realize your true self, you will rest in the silence of your being and dissolve all sense of separation. Your true nature is always at peace and rest behind the projections of the personal self. Turning within, guides you to effortless being, nurturing the precious self that lives in the sanctuary of your heart.

The struggle to find the self in worldly identification is a long and arduous journey. This struggle, the root cause of suffering for humanity, comes to an end when the search for the self turns within, meeting the eternal self which is ever-present. It is the realization of your true nature within, that holds the key to your truth in life, setting you free from all illusions. As you let go of all effort and struggle to become something outside of yourself, you will discover that your inner God-self is abundant with joy, peace and love.

Within you, is a sacred being that you can trust, listen to and receive guidance from, throughout life. Know this sacred self is always present, see yourself as a whole being, free from bondage of the conditioning of this temporary world.

The true self is pure awareness, untouched by all conditions and lives in mastery of what obscures this awareness. When you know yourself deeply as you truly are, all things observed in the knowledge of your true self will be immersed in the heart of your true vision. This true vision when clear, like a pond undisturbed by the ripples, will reflect the light of your being. The pond of your soul when disturbed reflects the ripples created by the personal self, striving to maintain its separate identity.

As you move deeper and deeper into stillness, the light of your soul will shine clearly, illuminating your path home. You will become disengaged from your ego-self, and see clearly that its illusion, is the cause of sorrow. In your natural state of observation, you are at rest and peace, remaining detached and strong to whatever appears in your life.

See deeply that you are in essence the embodiment of God; all things that come into the light of observation, can be healed by this looking. Impressions of the past and projections of the future will display in the quiet of your true nature. Remain steadfast in your truth and wisdom, because your essential nature is in reality free from the past and the projection of the future. The light of your true self has great discernment between passing thoughts and what is your true wisdom.

Trusting, in what is always present and at peace within, is to be free from the patterns of desire that are so imbedded in the conditioning of thought. Know that when you retreat into your true nature, you will find a beautiful and sacred being, free from all impressions.

Sorrow is the result of believing in your separate identity and spending a lifetime trying to uphold that. With grace, it is possible to discover that it is the ego nature of our beings that has lead us astray. We learn that it is the ego-self that projects fear, constantly searching to uphold its misidentification. This fear is the basis of all conflict and separation, for when the ego-self dissolves into the pure consciousness of stillness, the love of your true nature is revealed.

Turning your attention within requires a letting go and accepting the light that you are, this is where the listening begins. In listening, you have the opportunity to hear the song of your soul which is pure love. All things not of this love come from the separation that is created from fear and from the identification with thought and accompanying emotions.

Your true reality is one of eternal peace and love. When peace and love are lacking, observe the personal nature of your life. Observe where the personal investments lie, what you are trying to uphold, and what you are trying to run away from.

Remember throughout all changes, within you is your ever-abiding eternal self, unaffected by outward change.

As you surrender to your true nature you will have the inner strength to face all that appears in your path. Your true nature which is pure love and wisdom, is always present, seeing clearly the truth of your life. Letting go into your natural peace and ease of being, brings lightness to your life, knowing deeply that this manifested reality is just passing in time. You reach a greater understanding of your true nature, releasing all conditioning and programming from the past. Your eternal reality is not subject to time, or the process of birth and death.

The sacred is found in the heart of your being, where you find the peace of your ever-lasting nature. Your true self is closer to you than your very breath, the very beat of your heart, it is you in your simplest form. The beauty of your true essence is revealed when thoughts and emotions are calmed. In your quiet, you are able to listen to the voice of silence, the wisdom of your true nature. Understanding who you are, in truth, will guide you to a natural ease of being, where the trust, and wisdom of your true self is expressed. This understanding comes from the inquiry into your true nature.

The journey begins when you venture into the silence of being, where all answers are found. On this most sacred inner path, you must travel alone, free from dependency on outside sources. The pathway of heart, must be completely free from all authority, for when you follow authority you are lead into imitation, away from the source of your own inner light and wisdom.

You can observe how deeply conditioned the self is to seek the stamp of approval from outside sources. From an early age we are told we are good or bad according to the judgment of others, so life begins a cycle of imitation. The sacred self within, is rarely met, listened to or nurtured.

Conditioning is the root cause of misidentification, where the belief that we are the body, senses, emotions, and the thinker of thoughts is so embedded in our nature. We create a separate individual within that lives life in pursuit of itself, rarely glimpsing our true nature. The inner sanctuary awaits you through a simple turning within, and surrendering to your eternal presence.

Life is about mastery of the false and to live according to your inner truth. To begin, the personal self must take a back seat as the charioteer of your life. Mastery of the personal self, occurs when the light of your true being emerges and you live life in service to the divine. The master of your life is you; found when you retreat into the silence of your true nature. In this silence there is a possibility of communion with the sacred force of life where the self-centered programming of conditioning ends.

As you become more vigilant in disbelief of a separate individual, you merge deeper into the light of your true nature. It is through the return to the silence of the heart that you are able to discern the real from the unreal, seeing that the truth of being is pure eternal love. When there is silence, the personal self is one with the source of your being. This wholeness brings a deep peace to your life. In this silence you are free, sustained by the light of your true being. Your prayer is within you. The communion is a return to what is sacred and true, where the chalice of love awaits.

Remain ever vigilant and mindful of the workings of the ego-self. The master within, holds the sword of vigilance; use it wisely as the truth of your being. The master who lives in the silence of your being, is the charioteer to guide you safely home to the wisdom of the inner true self. Love yourself gently in this process and seek the compassion of your spiritual heart to assist you to see the workings of the false self.

Trusting in yourself is to live your life in devotion to your truth, knowing the inner life as your true reality. Trust is listening to the wisdom of the spiritual heart, merging with your divine nature.

THE ESSENTIAL QUESTION

The question "Who Am I?", is the most essential question for the purpose of self inquiry. It is essential not only to begin with the question "Who Am I?" but "What do I want?", in order to look into the heart of your truth for the answers. When the investigation of your true nature is tainted with strong personal desires for self-gratification, there can never be a sincere answer to this vital question. It may be more important to start with the inquiry of what you want from life, then it will lead to who you are in life.

This question will reveal the workings of the desire mind, which is obscuring the vision of your true nature. In life, we have the delusion of an apparent reality, what is seen and felt, and the strong illusion of the 'I' consciousness. The great mystery is behind all appearance; there is a stream of consciousness that is not dependent on anything. You are in truth this reality, a flowing consciousness untouched by the temporary nature of life.

The nature of desire is the deep conditioning that most humans suffer. We spend a life time seeking to fulfill desires, that are created by our self-centered programming. This programming is held deep in the conditioning of humanity, and must be questioned to begin the inquiry into the essential nature of life.

The simple truth is that self seeking has poisoned our life long enough, creating untold suffering in humanity. When you turn the attention from seeking outward gratification to the inner wealth of spirit, all desires are satisfied. Peace and happiness are found in abundance when you recognize your true nature.

The truth within all beings is one of radiance and beauty, not found in any outer circumstance. Touching upon your radiance, you will soon develop a passion to merge with your God-self. This is the fuel for your inquiry into the nature of your existence. The thirst for the eternal becomes a daily exercise in uncovering the veils that prevent you from this merging. Unifying with your sacred nature is the most precious endeavor of your life.

The inquiry into the nature of your life will lead you to uncover all that has been hidden in the recesses of your being. On behalf of freedom, you will see that nothing is real other than your eternal nature and the eternal nature of all beings. Once you realize the nature of your existence, all will be surrendered in the light of truth, liberating you from any residue of the past.

When you live in the investigation into the nature of the self, the veils that obstruct your true vision are lifted. What is revealed must be embraced and submerged in the light of your true radiant being. You will see the root cause of suffering in this world and compassionately look for ways to serve all beings.

The revelation of your 'true self' is the simple return to the source of your being, which is your sacred and divine nature. This revelation, is silence itself, which calms and brings peace to the process of thoughts and emotions.

Living a life of inquiry, leads you to turn within, where the living sage resides. The silence of your true self, is where emptiness becomes fullness and silence is the voice of wisdom. Recognizing your true nature, will uncover all that is not true, uncovering what you are not, leaving these accumulations from false identity behind you.

Insight into the vastness of your being will be your gift to yourself as you journey into the deep cavern of your heart. Inquiry is the tool that clears away the mistaken identity so deeply embedded by our conditioning. Look into the nature of your true self and all that you are not will fall away, as the immense light of your true nature is revealed. As you meet yourself completely, you will dance in the light and love of your being. This dance of your life will become a daily sacred celebration.

Your inquiry into the truth will reveal all that is not true; a simple letting go is all that is needed to release the false identity that has been created through time and memory. The intention, in finding out who you are is, in truth, a great yearning for the God-force within you. This yearning is a call from your true self, your divine nature. The sacred fire within transcends all behaviors, patterns, and destructive thoughts that are not aligned with your true nature. This sacred fire will create the path that leads you from unreal and to the real.

Look into what you are seeking from this life, if it is happiness and peace you seek, then know that it is found within the stillness of your true nature. When you investigate the question of who you are and what you want from life, you will uncover your true wish in life. All seeking and desires stem from the search for happiness. Discovering what you are not, will lead you to uncover your inner truth, the foundation for all true happiness.

The moment is where the true self lives, untainted by past impressions, whether they are pleasurable or painful. The moment is capable of great peace and love, from this place all is created. The moment is free from desires that are a product of time, it is unlimited happiness and bliss of being.

The personal self, along with its accompanying deep conditioning, has the habit of years and years of chasing thoughts and external desires. If you look deeply you will see that these desires and thoughts are never satisfied, leaving a lingering feeling of emptiness. There is no end to this seeking, no fulfillment of any desire. For the personal self is a bundle of thoughts and reactions based on memory, non-existent in truth. How can the personal self, which does not exist in truth, ever find fulfillment in seeking?

Live the questions of life that reveal the secrets to your eternal being; these questions are vital to uncovering the truth of your life. The personal self, will continually carry the reactions, attractions and repulsions of its self centered conditioning, resulting in pleasure and pain. Most human beings spend their life in this way. Waking up to this programming is to open the heart of compassion and question the reason for this birth. Through realization of the eternal self, you will begin to seek a balance from the outward gratification of the personal self, to turning within and nourishing your inner true self.

Inquiry into the truth of your being is the groundwork for letting go, and opening the path to your true nature. To begin, you observe the self-centered programming; the pursuit of self-gratification, resulting in satisfaction, then repulsion; a cycle that is repeated throughout your lifetime. See how the endless search for the self in pleasure, results in pain, and the wheel of cause and effect continues on for a lifetime. When you see that this is the way most humans spend their life, it ignites the fuel for self inquiry. The illusion that there is a personal self attaining something is deeply embedded in our thinking, we rarely turn within and experience our ever-present fullness. Discernment is seeing the pattern of desire, while turning the attention within to stillness and observation. This eagle vision will lead you to a greater intelligence in your life, seeing clearly and acting from the awareness of your true nature.

The realization that the personal self is not your true nature, opens the channel for the light of your truth and wisdom to shine. When the personal self is seen as the functioning self in service to the truth within you, there will always be a unity with your true abiding sacred nature.

The heart which is pure and free is the heart that is liberated from the past, creating a spaciousness of being, a passion for life. The deep feeling of the heart, is a heart that feels the pain and the joy of the world, while understanding the temporary nature of this passing time on earth. The deep feeling of the heart is our most sacred and profound guide, offering a map to our life's path. When we listen to our spiritual heart, we hear the wisdom of our own divinity. The true song of the heart is a song of great devotion to the eternal God-force within you.

In all walks of life, whatever position you hold, taking time to nurture your true nature is the greatest gift of self love. Your life and the roles you take on can be played out with a great more compassion, detachment, and understanding when you know deeply that you are not these roles or your conditioning. Within you is a sacred being, worthy of attention, respect, and honor; know yourself as this sacred being.

The veils that cover your true nature, are the many layers of belief in a separate individual. When you realize the self, the veils are lifted. As long as there is a belief in a separate person who lives life for the gratification of desire, the veils of separation will exist. When you return to silence of being, separation ceases, and the radiant light of your being is revealed.

Trust in this mysterious life of miracles and know that you are a part of the sacred energy of life. By deep understanding of your real nature, the wants and desires become a divine play in your life, but not seen as essential ingredients to bring you the peace and happiness you seek. Your true nature is peace and happiness, regardless of what has been attained.

Clarity of being is to live life with good intentions and to serve the purpose of the divine self within you. The divine self is your true and ever abiding nature, whose expression is pure love. The intention to live in your truth is to bring about a great love for yourself, and the divine yearning to end your personal suffering, and the suffering of all of humanity. If the intention is to truly meet the sacred, then you must end identification with your ego-self, returning to your true nature of pure being and peace. Silence, our sacred resting place, pacifies the emotions, the thoughts and the activity of the personal self. In the silence of your being, the wisdom of your heart opens to itself, bringing a vital force to you.

The illusion of the ego-self begins, by following thought and desire out for the purpose of self-gain. This way of being has its roots in separation and fear, where your true nature is veiled by the ego's willful, self-centered program. This creates an individual who lives a life of striving, thinking only about personal survival. Inquiry must be an ongoing process; investigating what lives behind the activity of the personal self. This may take you to the ruthless observation of the self and the programming that goes along with it. When the true self is realized, the love needed to bring your life back to wholeness becomes accessible. All separation and fear are dissolved in the love of your sacred self, the source of truth.

What you have gathered through thought and experience are just bundles of memory. The real "you" has never been defined by thought or memory; it is pure consciousness. The inquiry into your true nature leads you to uncover what is hidden by false identification. What is uncovered is the real essence of your being, no longer defined as separate, you fall deep into your eternal presence of infinite beauty.

The personal self engages in life and receives the consequences for all involvement, this involvement can be understood as your karma, the cause and effect of your actions. If you observe the personal self clearly, ending its self-centered program, you may be able to break this cycle. The work of your being is to surrender to the truth of life, grace will take you the rest of the way. Grace, is the great force that assists us to return to our divine home, the stillness of our being. The heart when set free from worldly identification, has a great space to open to the deep peace and silence of its true nature.

The art of observance is living in union with your true self, radiantly aware and present in this moment. This is the most beautiful expression of your being that you can ever know. When self consciousness is dropped, you enter into true meditation and communion with the divine, touching into great beauty. Your true essence in its most simple form is just pure witness consciousness, a partner with the divine.

The divine witness is your guardian angel within, clothed in great discernment, beauty and truth, on the throne of great love. Look within and see what is sacred, full of song, joy, wonder and divine inspiration. Release the burden of worldly identification, living in the world, but not of it. You are, in reality, a free being, regardless of the entanglements of the world. Let the inquiry into your true nature become a living, breathing question, moment to moment, revealing your true self.

Life is a drama in which we play many roles. When there is a deep realization that you are not the roles you play, your path to freedom opens. You see clearly that it is only through identification with the drama and the parts you play that is the cause of sorrow. We suffer immensely when we invest in these roles with our life essence, rarely glimpsing our eternal nature. We are caught in the web of time, in the process of becoming, and the effort of the personal will toward self-gain.

IS THIS THE MOST ESSENTIAL AND USEFUL WAY TO LIVE?

You see that by shifting attention toward your eternal nature, you can stop the endless cycle of personal suffering. Death becomes a great reminder that our time in this body is so precious. Inquiring into the nature of life, we see that most of life is spent believing in our external roles, rarely meeting our eternal nature. Investing in the eternal aspects of life is a rare opportunity, offering us a security that is everlasting.

We hold the key to awareness that can end needless suffering for ourselves and others, assisting the holy within to do its work without impediment. Abide in the only true reality; allowing your true self to emerge. This is a simple shift of attention from your known reality, to the unknown sacred force that is the river of life.

When the attention has shifted from what is your known identification to the eternal consciousness within, years of accumulated memory and sense of 'I' begin to crumble. As the grace of your true self emerges, all that you take yourself to be, your roles in life, your relationships, and your past will be seen as expressions in time. In your deepest knowing you will rest in the light of your eternal nature, touching into the infinite energy of the divine.

BEYOND THOUGHTS, EMOTIONS AND CONDITIONING

Within the realm of the personality lives conditioned thoughts and emotions that display in consciousness. Thoughts and emotions have a life of their own and will continue to appear and then disappear; this is the inevitable nature of your changing thoughts and emotions. Thoughts that relate to your functioning life are used as tools of your intelligence, to employ right action.

The nature of consciousness is observation, all is seen as passing clouds in the sky. Knowing that you are an eternal being, free from identification will allow all to pass freely in your consciousness. Following thoughts and emotions outward getting lost in their illusionary nature is the cause of the loss of self. Your true nature is always present, untouched by the what is seen This is the key to happiness, to recognize that you are free from the changing nature of life.

The work of the true self is to discriminate and discern between what is appearing and disappearing in consciousness. Upon observing the nature of thoughts and emotions, you can see that all thoughts and emotions come and go, but somehow there is always a part of you that does not change, that remains in witness consciousness.

Within your being is the unchanging nature of pure consciousness. The meeting with your true self, directly, without the interference of the activity of thought, is the answer to all personal suffering. This meeting, which is always present, is recognized when there is pure beingness, when all activities of the personal self are in silence.

A simple way of being is to know all passing states are temporary and to remain watchful, neither trying to run away nor trying to hold onto these passing states.

It is often the past scars and experiences that create deep tendencies of desire and repulsion. These tendencies, with their associated habits, will lead you to believe in your wounded self, seeking ways to correct this self. A greater awareness is necessary to observe the tendencies of your thinking and to see the source of these thoughts clearly. When the observer clearly sees that a little self has been created from thought and memory, you begin to question the reality of this individual. Seeing your true nature facilitates complete liberation from the past, bringing forth the love needed to meet any fear that arises from the separate self.

If you see that you are essentially a divine being, you can easily let go of the identification with the story of your life. When the reality of your true self is realized you are completely free from the past, the story and the possibility of the story continuing. The most courageous action you can take is realize the sacred eternal self that resides within your spiritual heart. By turning the attention from identification with the personal self to the truth of your sacred being, you are able to let go of your individual suffering. Letting go of individual suffering is the result of the love of your true nature, drowning the fear and separation caused by believing in a personal identity. It is the identification with the separate self, with years of memory that has created our false identity. When your attention turns away from the belief in who you think you are based on memory, to your sacred pure being that lives within, you will find freedom.

Fear is the holding of your identity in separation, finding comfort in the old familiar ways of belief in thoughts and emotions that keep you separated. Look inside to silence, perceiving the deep peace that awaits you in your spiritual heart. Your true nature which is pure love will dissolve all sense of fear and separation when you trust in that. Letting the personal nature of your life go, is to surrender to the ocean of your pure consciousness. Any self-consciousness or little wave beating upon the rocks will be dissolved in this process.

Your inner divinity will wash away all scars, all identity of the wounded, fearful self. In letting go, all conditioning is dissolved and purified by the fullness of your true nature. The consciousness of your life, is your true nature, the sacred river of your being. This sacred divine energy is the vital force of life, pure in being, free from content. Nothing that encompasses your worldly life can take away, touch upon, or change this divine consciousness.

Life's experiences lead you ultimately to the truth; for sorrow has its place in pointing you back to the nature of the true self, beyond identification with suffering. The root cause of suffering is revealed in the complete understanding of separation and misidentification. Finally, now all suffering can be seen as a great grace leading you to the awakening of your sacred nature.

In reality, your true nature is awareness and the embodiment of love and wisdom. Awareness is pure seeing with the love and compassion of the spiritual heart. Awareness and love make up the filter system for all thoughts and emotions. This creates a deep wisdom in the life of the self. This wisdom is your true and ever-present consciousness and, when activated, it transforms your life and completely heals the past, creating a holy relationship to each moment.

BEYOND CONDITIONING

You are in truth beyond all circumstance, events and the conditioning that has been imposed from outer circumstances, your true reality is that you are free from all outward affects. When you begin to inquire as to the nature of being, there is a look at your true nature without any conditioning at all. Through this process you begin to see that you are a pure and simple being when all conditioning and memory are cast aside. It is only through identification with our past and the conditioning that we create a false sense of who we are. Stop this identification and you will discover that there isn't a person who is bound by memory, and there is no suffering.

The eternal nature within, is our path to understanding life, and what lives on in truth. Turning to our eternal nature, opens the possibility to serve the truth of this birth for yourself and for other suffering beings. Death of the past, your identification with all that is temporary, is essential for deep and everlasting healing to take place. The scars from your past often leave deep impressions of sorrow. Knowing the true self will assist in the healing and release of impressions from these scars.

Your true self, in reality, is untouched by all past impressions. The most powerful tool you develop on this journey through life is to remain detached, aware of the changing nature of life. Know that at anytime you can retreat within to the light of your being, where all is observed from your truth, trusting in life's sacred movement.

As you become more familiar with the divine center of peace within, all is witnessed with detachment. No longer do you hold a personal investment in the story that unfolds before your eyes. You see the root cause suffering is the identification with the personal self, who is attached to the drama of life.

Your awareness of your true nature brings you to deeper and deeper levels of freedom. Freedom is your true nature, like a sacred beautiful swan, floating on the surface of the water with wings that never touch the water. This is the swan of our being, pure beauty and grace, walking lightly, leaving not a trace.

Dive deeply into your true everlasting nature and see the wounds of the past disappear in the fire of eternity. Carry nothing in your heart except the love of the divine, the source of all of life. Know yourself as this love.

See that all conditioning from thoughts and emotions as the web created from identification. Upon seeing this, surrender to the infinite reality and reclaim your birthright of freedom. Know that without identification there is no experience, just passing events. In deeply understanding this, you will learn the great art of detachment and witness consciousness, remaining in constant union with your divine self.

The inquiry into your true nature opens the door of inner knowing, where you can rest in your divine sanctuary, regardless of the changing nature of life. Our very core, our essence is pure awareness, capable of great understanding, acceptance and love.

In understanding your true nature, you will notice there is always a part of you that remains quiet, observing and deeply feeling. The work of the silence within is to remain awake, aware, and silent during the time of suffering and during the time of great joy. Knowing the outer is always subject to change, you turn within to find the source of the eternal. The divine center within, is your direct contact with infinite wisdom and balance; the key to your peace and happiness. In living from your divine center, you are able to participate in life, ready to serve, free from the distraction of personal sorrow.

All beings in this world, regardless of their position in life, are subject to great suffering and loss. We have the opportunity to view life as a sacred movement and learn to trust its inherent teachings. In trusting yourself throughout all changes, we learn to love during times of suffering, giving our attention to the moment. This attention to whatever life is offering is deeply healing, allowing you to embrace all of life's experiences whether they are painful or joyful.

Remaining in your pure consciousness is the opportunity for all of the hidden fears and conditioning from thought to surface. Trust in what comes to you and fully embrace this "medicine for your soul". Hold onto nothing as the conditioning from your past surfaces, remaining firmly planted in your true nature.

If you look with eyes of love and compassion, you will see how all life's experiences manifest to aid you back to your true self. Life, in this way, is a supreme miracle when you can view all as sacred assistance in returning to the holy in life. When looking at life from deep reverence, we see how all of life's occurrences have lessons in truth for each of us.

Observe the nature of our human condition, the strong investments that are made in behalf of this temporary life. Our lives are rarely spent turning within to what is true and ever-lasting. When the process of disengagement with the personal self begins, we wake up from a dream lived. The waking process begins as the inquiry into the nature of existence becomes a daily remembrance of the sacred in life.

When you are in identification with the personal self, memories are just fragments in time and are either painful or pleasurable. Peace is found finally in understanding that you are not bound by time, and that your place of rest is within your eternal nature. You will know deep inside that your reality is you are a whole human being, unaffected by experiences in time.

The art of retreating back into silence and witnessing the events of your life is essential to alleviate personal suffering. In your retreat, you will find a greater source of wisdom, an understanding of your true reality. All will be seen as divine grace, and the prayer will be to live in grace, no matter what comes and goes in the outward appearance of life.

The mind, when in divine order, has the great capacity for discernment and truth. The mind, reaches a saturation point from following the ignorant self for most of this precious life. Then, there is a time when a great vigilance appears to stop entertaining every thought and emotion getting caught in its familiar web. Upon seeing this clearly, you become a student of your eternal nature within, in a constant state of returning to this sacred source of peace and rest.

Human beings have been extremely damaged in growing up where consciousness is not sacred. Violence, abuse and conditions have embedded a deep sense of unworthiness. The violence of mankind has laid it seeds of suffering into all human beings. All children are born free from these conditions in their natural state of love and goodness. As life progresses, children become conditioned like the rest of humanity. Their natural state of love and goodness become buried behind the defensive posture that develops from this conditioning. Conditions of our parents and their parents, of society and of education all play a part in the development of a deep sense of unworthiness, self doubt, dishonor and loss of the sacred.

Each person has a different story of personal suffering. When listening to the personal story of our brothers and sisters, we begin to understand that although all the scenes are different, there are aspects of the story that are the same in all peoples lives, such as great loss, attachment, illness, old age, sickness and death. See all how all aspects of suffering are divine graces pointing back to truth and to the sacred understanding of life. Each of these occurrences, however painful, ultimately point to the eternal in our beings. Often, a great wisdom is developed when we find out who we are in the midst of suffering and learn to trust in that. Knowing and trusting in our essential nature is freedom, connecting us to unconditional vastness of being.

Looking at humanity as a whole we see the root of suffering stems from many individuals living in self-centeredness, blindly following one desire after another, in mistaken identity. This is the deep conditioning, that has its roots in lifetimes of belief in a separate individual. When you have the intention to be free from conditioning, there must be an awareness of all of life. There must be a very honest look at the illness of humanity that has resulted in great fragmentation, suffering and sorrow. In searching for the answers to your personal sorrow, how can we who are a fragment of humanity begin the healing process? This question must be looked at deeply, when inquiring into your true nature. There must be a vital looking at the conditioning and sorrow of human beings that has been in existence for all our known time. Returning to the awareness of your whole being, unbroken by personal sorrow, will radiate to the world. The whole being within you is where all actions stem from the intelligence, wisdom and compassion.

These God-given qualities will assist the whole of humanity, correcting the errors of conditioning.

When you meet your true self within, you will automatically let go of the false layers of conditioning. This happens because all of our conditioning is related to thought, which is related to fear. Upon meeting your true nature, all conditioning is dissolved in the love of your true abiding nature. In your truth, you will see that you are free from conditions of your life and that being deeply in love with the divine nature of life dissolves all fear, revealing the love of your true self.

TRUST IN THE LIGHT THAT YOU ARE

The light of your being is the part of yourself that speaks for the pure consciousness, eternal, unbounded and beyond the limitations of the 'I' state. Inquiry into your true nature opens your inner path to wisdom. All fulfillment is found by turning within and seeing the light that you are.

When life is lived with the illusion that you are a separate individual, there is often ignorance and suffering. In reality the essential nature of each human being is beyond the conditioning of personal self, not subject to the object of desire or repulsion. The original error in consciousness, is one of separation. The assumption stems from believing there is a separate person, constantly searching to fill the void of the individual. The simple truth is the person who claims to need an identity just has to turn the attention from outward looking to the inner where wholeness is found. Self-realization occurs when you simply look within and meet the true self of your eternal nature.

When the mind is in a state of unrest it constantly projects outward following thoughts and emotions creating a web of illusion. In an effort to satisfy this restlessness, desires and the fulfillment of desires become the sole objective. A mind that gives way to all thoughts, desires and sensations is a mind that is a slave to the separate, ego-self. The mind that returns to silence has the great skill of witnessing, with the ability to discern what is real and what is unreal. This relationship of the mind and the sacred, brings an immense amount of love, vitality and wisdom to your life. In this state of silence, there is a restful and complete abiding in your true essence. Silence is the direct source of divine wisdom and divine love, found in the temple of your heart.

The art of observation and inquiry into the essential nature of life leads you to the understanding of the cause of suffering and separation in our world. Separation, power, and striving are the root causes of conflict in our inner world and the outer world. From the beginning of your lifetime, you are conditioned to uphold and strive to maintain your separate self in the world. These beliefs set the stage for a whole lifetime, leaving very little time for inquiry. Through the guidance of grace, you stop to question the meaning of this existence, looking into the nature of the true self. As the conditioning from the external falls, what is uncovered is your divine spark, the sacred essence of all beings. This requires a deep study of yourself. Through this self inquiry, awareness of that which is true, will reveal itself.

All beings have within them the spark of divinity where the inner wisdom of the sacred is accessed. In the light of your pure consciousness, there is wholeness, and the unification with the sacred and all beings. Your inner light will reveal to you the oneness of all of creation. In the absence of the personal self, you celebrate the freedom of your true nature, opening the heart to the song of the soul.

Meditation on "The Light of Spiritual Heart"

 As you rest in the stillness of your true nature, breathing deeply, see all thoughts and emotions as flowing through the emptiness of your consciousness. Breathing in, allow your attention to turn inward, back to the source of your thoughts and emotions. Breathing out, letting go, of all that prevents you from entering your divine home of stillness. As you deepen your attention inward, remembering the essence of your being, you will rest in your true essence of peace.

Breathing in, softly with compassion and gentleness, you will find yourself going deeper and deeper into the silence of your true nature, your spiritual heart.

Within your silence you will observe all that appears and disappears like floating clouds in the sky. Remaining untouched by what is seen.

Deepen your attention into the silence of your consciousness, you hear the sound of the universe, a song of eternal peace. The silence within brings you to a deeper understanding of what is, pure peace and love of being.

Journey into the quiet sanctuary of your spiritual heart, finding the wellspring of all the love, wisdom and understanding needed for your journey home.

Reality is simply the loss of the ego.

Destroy the ego by seeking its identity.

It will automatically vanish and reality

will shine forth by itself.

RAMANA MAHARSHI

CHAPTER TWO

LOVE

Love, the Sacred Chalice of Life
Living in Harmlessness
Compassionate Seeing
Meditation: The Sacred Chalice of Love Within.

LOVE, THE SACRED CHALICE OF LIFE

Love is seeing the truth in yourself and in others, understanding all is one. Love is inclusive without judgment, accepting and embracing all. In embracing all, we learn to live without judgment, with total acceptance, loving all that appears, loving this mysterious changing reality. For in loving "what is" there is an immense freedom to be of service.

Most beings hold in their hearts hidden hurts, fears and identification with the past. In this way, we are never free to live in the moment, free from wounds of separation. To apply the sacred force of love within is to deeply witness, where the memories and painful scars are held. In this divine witnessing, the transformation of your separate identity occurs and there is a merging with truth of your whole being.

Your consciousness is pure love, a witness to all things, when there is silence within, all is seen without attachment. Knowing deeply that misidentification is the root cause of all human suffering, you can observe in the light of service, surrendering all to your eternal energy. In silence, the conditioning from the past surfaces, where healing takes place in the light of your pure consciousness.

Where there is personal sorrow, love is hidden by the veils of the illusion of suffering. Suffering calls for the attention to areas in life where love is lacking, requiring one to reach into the spiritual heart of truth, applying love where needed. In loving ourselves, as well as others, we gain the ability to uncover all that is false, living in conscious union with wisdom and truth.

True love in the light of pure consciousness is to remain in your divine center free from the pulls of opposites, seeing that real love is not the opposite of hate. Love that is free and pure is love where one has no personal investment, looking for the fruits of love. It is love where there is no separation, seeing all as divine and serving the purpose of divinity and truth.

Love that is free and pure, expressed from the your inner true nature radiates the force and the clear energy of truth. Love is looking at whatever is appearing from a place of witness consciousness, knowing that the silent mind, when applied to each moment, is the most profound act of love that can of be given. The silent mind expresses the impersonal force of love, where there is no activity of the personal self, trying to attain, change, or reject. Love applied from the silent mind is attentive to the fact of the moment. Attention comes from the silent mind, that is completely free from the past, alive in the moment.

Love is the attention given to any moment, when attention is lacking, love is also lacking. This attention in which the ego-self is not invested, will result in right action, right speech and the fruits of the pure energy of love.

Love, in the deepest sense, is to give up all caring from the personal point of view. In personal love there is always a motive, a need, a becoming of the self in relationship to love. Love is the internal organic response to life, the action of bringing your life into the light of your pure consciousness, where there is freedom.

Love is the absence of projection into the future, instead it is living in the moment, honoring the sacredness of what is. Love is asking yourself "What do I want?" This question unravels the deep patterns of desire and personal motives, uncovering any obstacles to the meeting of your true essence, love itself.

Love is understanding that at the root of desire one usually finds the quest for peace and happiness. Love is turning your attention from outer looking, to looking within where you tap the unlimited love of your being. In this profound understanding the desiring for anything stops; going within you find complete contentment and joy. The source of peace and happiness is within you.

Trust in Yourself, for you hold the chalice of the of love within your being. Love is accessing your eternal wisdom and applying it to each moment.

Unconditional awareness and seeing without a personal motive is the essence of love. In this seeing, you allow yourself and that which is seen total freedom. Freedom, in this sense, is not freedom to do as one wishes for personal gain, rather it is a deep release of the identification with the false self. Love is spending this life in healing the false self, surrendering all to your inner light.

In the light of your pure consciousness one may enter nakedly, leaving all facades behind. Hold onto nothing as you return to the essence of truth that you are, for the love of your being will sustain you forever more. Inward flowering brings many beautiful and intricate blossoms, when nurtured by the divine love of your true nature.

Love is not sentimental, as sentimentality is the personal attachment to memories of your past experience seeking ways to recreate them. Love is skillfully using your higher mind, seeing each moment anew. Love is not possessive; for the true love is not based on owning anything, rather love is having the intention for freedom for all beings, our sacred birthright.

Love is the essence of your pure consciousness. Love that has evolved past the personal state is the purest love that you can apply to the moment. Love that stems from the depths of your heart and the clarity of your higher mind is love that is integrated. Love is complete trust in the source of all creation.

Love, from your deep conditioning, is based on your self-pleasure. If pleasure is given, you continue to love and if not, there is rejection. The never ending cycle of fulfilling your empty self continues on in life until one day, there is a great urgency to stop, and wake up. The love of your true being is found deep within the heart, and becomes your most sacred guide when accessed. Through turning within, all separation and self motives end in the brilliance of your true nature, which is the pure love of consciousness. Bring all sorrow of the heart to this wellspring of love, surrendering all of your self motivated actions in this sacred spring. It is here where all love is purified to reflect the light of the divine. There is no more separation when you have turned and witnessed the divine truth of love within, all individuality disappears in the power of this truth.

Love is the jewel of the heart that is waiting in its complete radiance to be discovered. This love, discovered within the spiritual heart, is given freely without images and conditioning of the past, or fear of future outcomes. The love within the spiritual heart, resides in the hearts of all beings, creating a profound oneness in life.

Love is the fire of truth, to be used to uncover the ignorance in your life. It is the force that is behind the sword of vigilance, seeing through the veils that hide your true nature. Love is anger applied that is correct, based on your truth, courageously seeing where attention is needed. Love is living the truth in your life and applying the virtues of discernment, righteousness, awareness, discipline, vigilance and nobility to the moment. These gems of the mind are the very precious jewels on the crown of love.

Love is turning to the eternal wellspring of the spiritual heart, bringing forth the love that is needed for your daily life. It is the courage to except the challenges of life, knowing that the source of all strength and love is found in the wellspring of your spiritual heart. When the higher self, or impersonal self, engages in love there is an essence of freedom and unconditional acceptance. The love of your true nature sees no separation, no individual person who is giving or receiving love. The true love of the aspirant of freedom is to assist all others in becoming free, released from personal sorrow. The love of your pure consciousness is a celebration of freedom and the divine in all beings. When you taste the nectar of love within, there is a dropping away of all that is not of this freedom, spreading your wings to fly in truth.

Love shared from the light of pure consciousness is love of the divine, beyond personal gratification. Love from this sacred source is the supreme demonstration of wisdom, compassion, forgiveness, acceptance, kindliness, harmlessness and generosity. Love is clear seeing of the truth and applying right action to the moment. Love offers you the key to your Christ nature within, uniting with the sacred.

In the silence of the heart and mind, love is allowed to flow freely from your divine source. This love is the wellspring of your true eternal nature. In sacred quiet of your spiritual heart, love is unbounded, and infinitely abundant for your sacred life. Within, your being is the living chalice of your divine energy, always overflowing when you tap into the eternal river of love.

Love is allowing your true nature to guide you in all walks of life, becoming the charioteer on your journey home. It is love that sets you free to live your life in truth. It is the sacred love of your being that is the nectar of the divine lotus within, ever-unfolding in the heart of your being. The sacred essence within stems from the divine source of love, from which all things come. Life is a constant return to this eternal wellspring, where peace and silence is found.

Love is a great unifier for all things separate, all things in duality. Upon returning to the ever-present well-spring of love, all separation ceases, only unity and wholeness remain. Love is honoring the sacred quest to return to your natural state of silence within, resting in the wholeness of your true nature.

A great love for mankind is to see all others for who they really are, divine beings in the process of remembering. The greatest assistance and love we can give to all souls is to see them as ourselves, with great understanding and compassion. Love is the time in life where there is complete unwillingness to entertain the illusion of needless personal suffering.

Trust in Yourself, you are an instrument of love, beyond sorrow, beyond conditioning and beyond time and memory. This life is the opportunity to play the tune of your sacred song of love, in rhythm to the divine melody within your spiritual heart.

LIVING IN HARMLESSNESS

When there is complete identification with a separate individual who lives life in behalf of ego-identity, there is a great division and fragmented way of being. We live our lives projecting our self-needs, seeking and repelling, in search of validating our ego-self. The life of the false self is a fragment of the whole, contributing to the endless and needless suffering of humanity. This is a state of turmoil, that creates lifetimes of sorrow for most human beings.

As we become more and more aware of our true nature, our responsibility deepens and we can no longer live a life in service to our ego-self. We see that by becoming whole within directly effects all of humanity. A deep understanding develops, turning your attention inward to the eternal peace of your inner truth. Turning within takes you to the depth of your spiritual heart where it is possible to see all is one. Within the heart a great compassion emerges, where you see that all suffering stems from division and fragmentation. Each human life is a reflection of the whole, making it vitally important for individual transformation. As our human nature transcends the limitations of the personal self, the whole of the world will be affected.

Living in each moment where your consciousness is awake, is living in harmlessness, the work of a true spiritual pilgrim. For when you are conscious of your relationship to each new moment, there can only be love applied. When there is an unconscious relationship to each moment, you are operating from the lower impulses of the personal self. A simple turning your attention from the personal self to the impersonal divine self, reveals the love of your inner divinity.

Harmlessness is the aspect of life where you operate from wholeness and the love of your inner truth. Harmlessness is a softness of being, a surrender of self needs for the goodness of all concerned. Harmlessness is offering yourself to the service of the moment while giving up the desperate attempts for self-gratification, letting life unfold in its natural process of beauty, truth and love.

Living from your true self, there is unlimited access to the wisdom found within, resulting in clarity, love and right action. In trusting your true nature, you are never alone, while walking the path of this temporary world. The presence within is always offering assistance, in all ways, the light of the world is your light.

COMPASSIONATE SEEING

Compassionate seeing is to observe life with an unconditional heart and open mind, accepting all in the flow of consciousness. In this way of seeing, there is total honesty, total acceptance of "what is" and a possibility of transformation. Allowing all thoughts and their accompanying desires to surface without running away from or holding onto them, keeps your channel clear, remaining in pure consciousness.

Surrendering to your spiritual heart, is the way of the compassionate spirit, your path of divine love. When you learn to observe with the eyes of compassion, what is seen is brought into the light of truth. Compassionate seeing is to live in complete acceptance as to how things are, seeing the changing nature of life, while knowing the real, eternal force that is behind this changing reality. When compassion is applied, you are able to see the suffering of others with a heart of service, walking in the light of your true knowing, sharing this light with all.

In seeing with the wisdom eye, the doorways to your inner truth open, touching upon the mystery of life. This brings about an understanding of and the ability to disengage from identification of what appears in the moment. This seeing without identification is the real act of love applied, allowing for the ever-evolving truth to reveal itself.

Compassionate seeing is to see yourself in truth and clarity, deeply surrendering all attachments and desires of the personal self. Living in compassion is to see yourself and others as the embodiment of peace itself. Seeing with compassion is to view all of your personal motives and tendencies for self-gratification, accepting them fully, surrendering them to the fire of compassion. Observe, that your true essence is love of a much higher nature, and your true happiness is found when you are living in service to your truth.

Compassion is to understand the suffering process in yourself and others. The love within you, when exercised, has the ability to heal the deepest afflictions of spirit. This love fills the empty cup of all searching souls. We spend most of our lives looking through eyes of desire and want, veiled in the ignorance of the personal self. These eyes when deluded by our personal nature, have a great mist blinding us to "what is." This mist is the sum total of our accumulated desires and wants. This veil of deception, clouds our seeing with images, thoughts and projections of the false self

Compassionate seeing, is to observe the tendencies of the personal self, mastering it with the fuel of the wisdom of the heart. When the force of the divine witnessing lifts the veil, a great freedom of being is revealed. A profound commitment to seeing the truth develops, preventing the veils of the false self from ever developing again.

Witnessing from your inner truth, and the heart of compassion effects your daily life by bringing beauty and transformation to all you touch. You learn to see yourself and others unconditionally. Love applied unconditionally is the supreme balance of love and wisdom, resulting in responses that stem from your divine intelligence. Each new moment is a new opportunity to apply the love and compassion needed for what your life is manifesting. Living in the moment with compassion requires a letting go of the past with all its images, memories and impressions.

Compassionate seeing is to look at your family and friends as they are, without denial, see their calling, their yearning and beyond their fragmented souls. Compassionate seeing is to see the roots of suffering with great understanding and love. The action of compassionate seeing is to look dearly, carefully with a heart that accepts and loves unconditionally, seeing the core of truth in all.

In seeing with your wisdom eye, there is a deep understanding that life's passing events, are just a part of the play in the drama of life. The roles you take on in the drama of life will never define your true eternal nature. You begin to feel a sense of joy and lightness, when you know that you are not these roles. A compassionate heart, is your inner guide to the pathway within, where you will find all the nurturing needed for your journey. Voyage within, to the deep wisdom of your spiritual heart, where your true self dwells. Upon entering into this ever-deepening vastness, you will meet the eternal presence who will be your companion, guide and master throughout all experiences of life. Trust in your inner true self, the light of your being and the light of the world.

Meditation on the "Sacred Chalice of Love Within"

Go quietly into the depth of your spiritual heart and observe what lives there, without the distraction of pulling thoughts and emotions.

This quiet sanctuary of your being is your resting place, where you may receive the nourishment from the source of all love.

This place of rest is the Sacred Chalice of Love found in your spiritual heart. It is here that you receive the nourishment of love, wisdom, and compassion for all of life's challenges.

Bring to this wellspring of the heart any concerns, worries, or challenges and offer them to the sacred cleansing water of your being, dissolving them into stillness and perfection.

The Sacred Chalice of Love within is the eternal medicine of the soul always available to nurture, mend, and align you with the perfection that you are.

Be cleansed of the self's features,

and see your pure Self: behold within your heart all

the sciences of the prophets, without books

and without a teacher.

RUMI

CHAPTER THREE

YOUR ESSENTIAL NATURE

Your Essential Nature
Living Beyond Your Known Identification
Doubt, the Obstacle to Trust
Meditation: Your Sacred Essence

YOUR ESSENTIAL NATURE

Your essential nature is always present, but veiled by projections of the personal nature of the self. When you are tired of experiencing the story that the personal self creates, the path of return to what is true begins. All that is needed is to turn within, and recognize the sacred being who is always present. When this recognition happens, you have taken the path to freedom and the ever-lasting wisdom of life.

In the pure consciousness of your truth, you are just quiet, relaxed and in your natural place of peace. In surrendering to the quiet within, you stop indulging in the countless thoughts and emotions that appear and disappear in consciousness. Witnessing becomes your second nature as you naturally see all as a changing part of the unfolding drama of life. Life is no longer taken so seriously as you step out of the concrete hold of identification. There is a lightness in your being, bringing laughter and joy, and finally the understanding that you are not the person directing this whole display.

The essential nature of all human beings is one of vastness, luminosity, boundlessness, and eternity. Just being, surrendering into your essential nature, will assist all efforts of the personal self. Letting go is the activity of your true self, as it merges with its true divine nature, deeply realizing that it is not fragmented or separated from the source. You are in reality, the observer of all things, silently observing and remaining detached as all comes and goes in your view. You are the master of your life and in clear seeing you choose your dream, creating a story of untold beauty.

You are the witness of all, remaining absolutely silent, untouched by the impermanent nature of life. Surrendering to your spiritual heart liberates you from the illusion of bondage, in your freedom you ascend to infinite understanding of the sacred in life. Allow all things not of your essential nature to be immersed by the powerful witnessing that is your daily life. Your essential nature, is a pure witness to the experience of life, discerning the real from the unreal. Life in this way is a joyous dance with the sacred force that is behind all manifestation.

Upon investigation into the truth of your being, you see that you are undefined and unbound to any beliefs or authority. Inquiry is the path to the endless revelation of your ever-evolving, true nature. When the identification shifts from the self that is based on time and memory, to the emptiness of the self, a complete transformation of life occurs. When you end measuring your life with time, you will meet your timeless essential nature. You will discover that all belief, images, and conditioning are rooted in time and that your true essential nature resides out of time. Your essential nature is calling you to return to your natural state of unbounded light. You can look within your deepest heart's desire and feel this calling. This calling is to return to what has always been present within, the beloved presence in your spiritual heart.

When you move into the silence of your being, you will discover that there was never a journey away from the spiritual heart, only a temporary distraction of thoughts and emotions. When you are firmly planted in witness consciousness there is no longer this distraction, just pure awareness of the emptiness of your true nature. All separation is dissolved in this vast ocean of your being, the ego-self merges with the your true sacred essence.

Surrendering to your sacred nature within is to let go of all striving and outward manipulation. Letting go is simply relaxing into your true nature, where there is complete freedom, and totality of being. In the midst of this journey the personality becomes exhausted from all effort. When the self that is identified with this changing reality reaches the end and looks back to its sacred source, the search is over. A doorway opens to the source of consciousness and this consciousness floods the ego identification. The ego identification, or personality, becomes fully in service to the beloved within, your true divine nature.

Your inner being is a sacred force, clothed in temporary garments, untouched by all memory, all experiences in time. Living in your true essential nature, moment to moment, is to be firmly embedded in witness consciousness, seeing all as part of the passing drama of life. Your true self is accessible and verifiable as you turn your attention within to the silent force of your divinity. The silence of your being, is where you meet your inner-most self, and take the journey to infinite truth.

Observe the function of the physical body clearly, the temple of your sacred being. In this clear seeing, you will cherish this most sacred temple, with great love, respect, and honor. Observe your emotions as gateways to the deep feeling of your soul. In this way, you will experience the truth of your being with great love. Observe the mind as the vehicle for great understanding and allow the mind to soar to the edges of eternity. When the mind reaches this vastness, it rests in silence, surrendering all effort to the unbounded source of pure consciousness. This divine source is the sacred temple of your spiritual heart.

BEYOND YOUR KNOWN IDENTIFICATION

The lotus has its roots in the mud, with its ever unfolding petals that reach into the sky. This is a deep analogy of our spiritual life, a way to be in the world but not of it. We walk in the beauty of our un-folding, knowing that each step is a light one, tentatively walking the path of this temporary existence. In living beyond our known identification, we know that we are temporarily inhabiting this body but not of this body. We are in this world but not of this world. We see all things of this world as temporary and endeavor to know the eternal aspects of life. The nature of change teaches us that impermanent aspects of life are subject to death, while our eternal nature lives on, untouched by outward change.

Our known identification has shown us that which is limited, temporary, and transient in nature, subject to great suffering, loss, and death. What is known is subject to time and the conditions of this temporary world. When you venture to live beyond what is known, there is a possibility of touching the eternal, unknown, mysterious reality. To live beyond your known identification requires a great courage and willingness to explore the vastness of this magnificent universe, treading the path of the infinite.

Live beyond your known identification, and open to your unlimited potential, reach into the core of your essence to see what is revealed. You are a beautiful unfolding flower, ever-blossoming into your natural beauty and sacred nature.

SELF DOUBT, THE OBSTACLE TO TRUST

When we fall into self-doubt, we revert back to the belief that we are a separate, individual with its related story of personal suffering. We forget that our true essence is found by the simple turning away from belief in passing thoughts of unworthiness. Our thoughts when mixed with emotions, creates an inertia that is often hard to overcome, feeling the weight of worldly identification. The result is a deep feeling of fear in relationship to life, and the sense of being alone in our separate reality. This is the activity of the "I" self, indulging in its separate sense of reality. The illusion of a separate individual must be mastered by the light of your true nature.

The separate sense of self only exists in the context of time and memory. This can be easily verified if you stop and look for your-self, upon looking, you will not find this person anywhere. The definition of who you are is only found in conditioning through memory and time. Stand alone, without conditioning or memory and you will see that the personal self that you take yourself to be, doesn't exist.

The deep feeling of self doubt is rooted in the misidentification of your separate identity. Upon letting go of this misidentification, you meet your true self, the sacred self of all beings. Your true self is unbound by any condition and is free from time and memory. The sacred force lives within your being connects you to all of life, for in reality, you are this sacred force.

In truth, life is a living eternal essence of which we are a part, changing forms but remaining one continual consciousness. In reality there is no fear, it is merely an expression of your temporary nature identified with itself. Your true nature is the essence of divine love, which dissolves all fear. When you turn your attention inward, you will recognize your true nature, reclaiming the strength within your divine self. You will trust in the truth of your divine self, dissolving all misidentification of the personal self into your sacred nature.

Living in a state of doubt leads you to avoid the challenge of living in your true nature, whole and complete. This avoidance comes from a deep lack of self-worth which stems from the belief in yourself as a separate individual. As you begin to trust in your true abiding nature there will be a complete letting go of the identification with separation.

In the effort of trying to find ourselves in the world there is a sense of loss that grows deep within our heart. There is often a feeling that our life is being used on behalf of worldly expectations, and the real meaning of life is not revealed. We generally feel very drained and exhausted before we let go and ride the powerful current of our external being back to its sacred source. There is an inner calling that we have not followed, a sense that there is a loss of yourself somewhere in time. When the awakening of your true self occurs, this sense of loss disappears as the search for the self ends. What has been awakened is your selfless, eternal nature unbound by time and memory.

As the identification with the passing events of the temporary nature of life becomes disengaged, the true meaning of life is revealed. We can put the results of this birth into prospective and see the truth of our lives. All life events are seen as gifts and pointers to guide our lives to the divine. There becomes an understanding of your true self, seeing its eternal, unchanging nature. Through knowing the eternal nature of life, the illusion of a separate individual with all its related expressions, infinitely dissolve into the truth. The eternal nature of your being dissolves all feeling of self doubt, the obstacle to your true self. A lighted path is waiting for you to walk back to your true self of pure consciousness. This pathway is readily available by turning consciousness back to its sacred source. Inquiring into your true nature lights the pathway for your return home.

Meditation: Your Sacred Essence

Relax into the your sacred essence, the light of your spiritual heart.

Bring your attention inward, observing any thoughts or emotions as a passing wind in your pure consciousness.

Breathing deeply, bring your awareness to the sacred essence within your being, returning to the stillness of your true nature.

As you remain in stillness, you sense a clear pond of sacred energy. This sacred pond within, reflects the peace of your inner being as you deepen your awareness in your spiritual heart.

Resting deeply in the light of your spiritual heart, the ripples of your sacred pond are becoming absolutely still. You are now able to reflect upon the radiance that you are, the sacred essence of the divine.

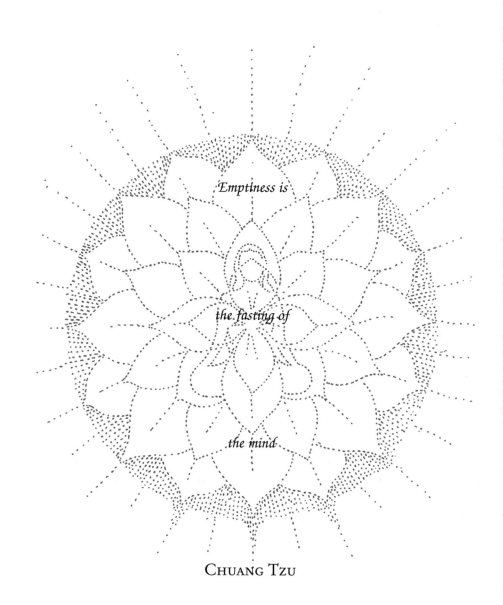

Emptiness is

the fasting of

the mind

CHUANG TZU

CHAPTER FOUR

FREEDOM

Attachments, Bondage and Personal Desire (seeds of suffering)
Living your Sacred Journey
The Disappearance of the Sufferer
Meditation: Your Sacred Journey

ATTACHMENTS, BONDAGE AND DESIRE (SEEDS OF SUFFERING)

Please inquire as to the nature of suffering. What is it that truly suffers and what remains quiet, calm and in a state of peace? What is suffering other than a state of separation and misidentification?

Suffering of the personal one is a result of the 'I' consciousness not fulfilling the planted seeds of desire. What comes will never quench the thirst of the empty personal self. In reality there is not a separate individual achieving desires, being satisfied and forever being contented. There is in truth, no separate individual who achieves anything at all. It is all a product of thought which is projected onto life.

Desires that stem from the mind are a product of thought, never manifesting what the restless mind projects. Desire is a great reveler of the content of your consciousness, leading to the awareness of what you truly want from life. Observation of the desire self is honestly looking at your patterns and tendencies, from past impressions. The inner work for the person seeking freedom from illusion, is to observe the subtle tendencies that keep you from truth, allow them to surface while remaining in silent witness consciousness. Past, present and future become one under the healing transformation of divine observation.

The human condition is to spend life devoted to temporary accumulation and the satisfaction of desire, very rarely glimpsing the eternal. It is only through inquiry into the truth of life, that you begin to turn within to find ever-lasting happiness and peace. When thoughts and emotions are stilled in the light of your pure being, peace becomes the foundation for your life. The invitation from the eternal nature within is to retreat into the light of your pure and divine consciousness where all is immersed, leaving no residue of personal suffering.

By ceasing unnecessary suffering, we have the strength to face the innate suffering of the life and death process. It is urgent that we begin to see the suffering of the world, and look within the heart to be of service. This requires the study of the self in relationship to desire, seeing that all desire has its roots in the separate ego-self.

The strong will of the personal self is convinced it has a life of its own, never reaching the end of its projected needs, never tires when it is fed by worldly gain. Suffering ends when your plate is full with disillusionment, seeing clearly that all effort to fill your desires usually ends in great loss and disappointment. When your life ends the course of self-gratification, there is a natural turning within, to ever-lasting divinity. A great yearning and devotion develops to the living truth within, where all fulfillment is found.

In the quietude of our hearts and minds we fall deep into our sacred home of emptiness, where our personal wants and desires are no longer in power. We see that in truth our essence is eternal, and the manifestation of our being into physical form, holds nothing while walking in the eternal light of the divine. This temporary walk on this fragile earth becomes a walk in devotion to the realization of God, and the eternal divinity that lives within all beings.

The search for your true nature leads you to let go of all desires and attachments that keep you from finding freedom. In reality your true nature is always free, but the veil of the personal self is preventing you from fully experiencing your unbounded eternal nature. When the veil is removed, there is a oneness of being, complete wholeness, and unlimited vitality to live in truth.

Desires of a self centered nature, when acted upon, bring a deep of loss, because our sacred energy goes to that which is non-existent in nature. The personal self is an empty well and will never be filled by the attainment of temporary pleasures and self-centered desires. When you turn within, the divine replenishes what is lacking, and all seeking ends. The life of desire, is to live life generally regretting what we don't have and looking for something better to fill our empty wells. We seek power and security in a powerless and insecure world, never finding an ounce of security as all attainments turn to ashes in the end. Our true stable ground is to dive into the eternal within, letting go of all identification with the search for security. Know that your essence is one with divine consciousness, lacking nothing and infinitely complete in truth.

Life is one of change and all outward manifestation is subject to the laws of nature. If we truly see that nothing in manifestation is permanent, we naturally move to that which is eternal, the unknown force of our life. Suffering and pain will come and go, as with joy and happiness. These are the conditions of this birth. Remain in constant center throughout all the changes, and see your unchanging eternal nature.

In truth and ultimate reality, you are a whole human being, unaffected by all outward changes. The awakened mind has inquired into the nature of existence and has discovered that suffering is the result of separation. This lifetime is an opportunity to discover what you are not; by turning your attention inward to the source of life. Know thyself and you will enter the kingdom of heaven where your eternal nature rests.

Your essential nature of goodness is like a sieve, allowing all to go through, and holding only that which is in service to your divine nature. Strengthen this sieve as you develop the jewel of discernment. Your true nature is one of love, goodness, and peace itself. Expressing these gifts of your soul is tending to the garden within, nurturing, and creating beauty and everlasting goodness. Your eternal nature is the pathway to the infinite, where you realize the vastness of being, bringing everlasting joy and peace.

Knowing your true essential nature, and trusting in that, is recognizing that your home is the emptiness of your pure consciousness, and this life and all its expressions be in service to that. Each moment that goes by in personal suffering contributes to the suffering of the world. Each moment spent in behalf of freedom and love of the divine will radiate out to the world. Understanding of your true nature, pure consciousness is essential to the peace of this world. The work of freedom is to no longer allow our human temporary nature, to taint this sacred life with its self-centered conditioning. The whole person within is complete unto itself, not dependent on the belief in a separate self who lives for self-gain and self-pleasure. Turning away from this deep conditioning, will change the world for we are each a part of the whole, the responsibility lies within.

Know deeply that your essential nature is one of great wisdom and you can simply be at peace with yourself. When you realize the true nature of your being, you will embark upon a journey of transformation, where the self lets go of the known reality and embarks upon the unknown path to the divine. Peace is absolute trust in your divine self, turning within to rest in the sanctuary of your silence. Open your wings, surrender to the winds of grace; you will be guided to freedom and peace of being.

Trusting in Yourself, the eternal aspect of your being, means you will spend your life in deep honor of your essential nature.

LIVING YOUR SACRED JOURNEY

Living your sacred journey is a conscious dance with the sacred force that moves to the rhythms of your inner song. This dance is a celebration of being that renews your natural joy and wonder. Your true nature is love and happiness and lives beyond the grips of the personal self. As you embark on the path to your true self, all obstacles on the path are gently removed. The sacred journey is the path to your inner wisdom, free from the encumbrance of thought that is based in time and memory.

Lifetimes have been spent in patterns of identification with the individual person on a journey of self-gratification. The journey now is to embark upon the new where you are able to walk the path with no past, letting life's mystery unfold. Living your sacred journey is to let go of anything that obscures the vision of your true nature. Your sacred path will set you on the course to your infinite and vast nature. You will discover the song of the heart and the lightness of being, experiencing untold joy as you touch upon the infinite nature of your true self.

On your journey you will let go of all things not of your truth, and assist others to understand the cause of suffering. You will see this sacred journey as most a precious opportunity to discover the eternal. Along your sacred path you will be guided by the angel of grace, who will point the way to the eternal peace of your inner divinity.

There are many signs along the way, look for the guideposts of effortless being, surrender, ease, rest, peace and deep love of truth. Open the doors along the way that deepen your understanding of your divine nature. Your sacred journey will lead you to understand the wisdom of life and it will point the way to peace, happiness and the compassion of your spiritual heart.

THE DISAPPEARANCE OF THE SUFFERER

The individual person, who comes into this life with certain tendencies and deep-seated patterns, continues to create more experiences in the complicated web of life. These tendencies, when unseen, can dictate your life and the choices you make from unawareness of your true nature. The wake-up call often comes about when you have experienced enough personal suffering and begin the liberating process of inquiry into the nature of the true self. This inquiry awakens the witness consciousness within, as the very nature of inquiry leads you back to the source of life.

In the process of inquiry, there is a revelation that you are no longer blinded by thoughts and desires that are displayed in your consciousness. This causes you to question and observe the blind and sleeping areas of your life, leading you to wake up to your inner being, the innate wisdom of the true self.

The ending of the sufferer comes from the deep and profound realization that the ego-self, masked as the real self, is in truth not your true nature. The ego-self is a product of the separate mechanism of seeking, forming deep patterns within your being. This habit is forever broken when there is the realization of the true self.

The true self of our beings, is layered beyond recognition through the deep conditioning of our lives. This conditioning, which is deeply rooted in our present way of being, is the cause of the sorrow of humanity. The identification with the outer appearance of life, is so strong that very little time is spent turning within, to our eternal nature. The loss of the true self usually begins early and continues on through old age, sickness, and eventually death. At death, consciousness is so identified with the body that there is little preparation for the meeting of the divine self, that which is formless and eternal. The invitation here is to look into the nature of your existence and meet the eternal spirit who lives within, forever resting in the light of truth.

The cessation of suffering is when you no longer believe in the story of personal suffering. The successes and failures in the world, the great losses or great gains, are just seen as what has appeared and disappeared. The identity remains with your eternal nature, your radiant light within sheds the light of detachment on the events of life, moving into a natural state of perception.

In observation of personal suffering from the viewpoint of divine witness, there is realization that you are completely free from identification with the story of life, deeply recognizing your eternal nature. There is no longer a belief in thoughts that define your identity. A great awareness develops, leading you to see beyond the illusion of the personal self, revealing the brilliance of your true nature.

In viewing suffering from detachment and witness consciousness, we see that through all of life's difficulties, there is always a great grace pointing back to your true nature. Life being a tough teacher, shakes up the very foundation of our life to guide us safely home. We pull back in fear when faced with a challenging situation, never looking to the real cause of suffering and the lesson of self. Seeing the truth of your life, looking for the lesson, is a taking responsibility for self involvement. Most often, the lesson will reveal that there is a desire at the core of the problem and that life is manifesting the lesson of that desire.

Inquiring into the nature of desire in life, is to apply your intelligence to the cause of suffering. Investigation must lead you to have the courage to see the nature of the personal self. Surrendering to the truth within, a strength and courage develops to see what is false. In reality, your true nature is not of this world and you no longer need to believe in outer appearances as a measure of your personal worth. You are free from all conditions, immortal and true, your only duty being the pursuit of your truth.

The suggestion is to look closely at the truth of the suffering. The root cause of all suffering is identification with memory, the past and the individual who is at the center of experience. When there is a detached look at life, you live in observation of where the identification lies, the root of suffering. The relief of personal suffering occurs when there is total responsibility for your involvement in the personal self.

The understanding that all of life matters and nothing matters is the paradox of living in the world with total attention and care, while also knowing that, in reality, nothing matters in reference to the changing nature of life. The identification with the sufferer disappears when there is complete realization of the eternal self, that is beyond the conditions of this physical manifestation.

Meditation: Your Sacred Journey

Journey within to your sacred resting place of stillness where the wisdom of your true nature is expressed.

It is in this place of wisdom that you understand the sacred nature of life, the eternal journey with no beginning or end.

You are pure consciousness that is moving through this temporary realm for the purpose of knowing your eternal self.

As you turn within, you will meet your innermost source, and you will see that all experiences begin and end in this source, leaving you to rest in the emptiness of your pure essence.

Kill the snake of desire in the beginning; or watch out:

your snake will become a dragon. But everyone considers

his own snake to be just an ant; if you do,

seek knowledge of your real state from one

who is a lord of the heart.

Until copper becomes gold, it doesn't know its copper; until the

heart becomes a king, it doesn't recognize its poverty.

RUMI

CHAPTER FIVE

MOMENTS IN ETERNITY

LIVING IN THE ETERNAL MOMENT

Living in the eternal moment is to recognize your emptiness, opening and expanding unto the fullness of your eternal light. Each moment is the opportunity, to know deeply that you are not bound by conditions of the past or future. Letting go is understanding the emptiness of self, knowing that in emptiness we find our true nature. When the heart is released from the sorrow of the past, it is capable of great love and wisdom. This heart is the spiritual heart of your being, the pulsating heart of eternity. The spiritual heart is the seat where your divine being is witness to all. The self when realized, awakens the heart to the infinite love of being and shines in its radiance.

The personal self has its roots in memory, this leads to the constant search to recreate the past or project into the future. When the personal self dissolves into the divine witness, the moment becomes alive with unlimited potential. The eternal moment, when lived fully, is free from the residue of the past, its impressions and scars. Each moment is an opportunity to remind yourself of the divine, letting go all veils to this truth. Each moment, offers you the opportunity to exercise the skill of letting go and allowing space for the new to enter. In this way, a great vitality of life is revealed as the weight of the past is lifted. This letting go is the art of surrendering within, to the living sage of eternal wisdom where life happens of itself.

The force of your true nature creates a shift in consciousness; turning your consciousness from the outer to the inner. The true nature of your self will wash away all that is not of your self, purifying your being from the core. The moment is the opportunity to live in truth, opening the doors to the divine mystery of life.

Each moment is a miracle with infinite possibilities to create the life you want, making this lifetime beautiful and sacred. You are constantly born "anew," to see clearly, to live clearly, and to give yourself to the next moment. Sorrow results when there isn't acceptance of the way things are, and when the past dictates and contaminates the new. Living in each sacred moment is living in the light of your true self and dancing with creation, accepting the nature of change. The moment is where the sacred presence is found, timeless and ever-lasting.

BLESSINGS ABOUND

You are an embodiment of blessings, a miracle of life. Your true nature is divine and holds unlimited potential and is infinitely free. Blessings are a natural occurrence in life, increasing your awareness of divine love. You are pure light blessed with all the wisdom, love, and the ability to know yourself as God. The only thing that is blocking you from this knowing is the veil of the ego-self. You are blessed beyond recognition, as your true nature is a reflection of God, with unimaginable beauty. You are blessed with a greatness, that is revealed when you look within and meet the sacred self that you are.

In your truth, you are pure joy, peace and unconditional love that is found in the silence of your being. Each day in remembrance of your nature, miracles are a natural occurrence. Your very nature is the embodiment of sacred life, the creative force from which all arises and disappears. Trust in your true divine nature, where all comes to peace and the healing light of love. Your true self weaves a tapestry of great beauty, unlimited possibilities, that arises from your pure consciousness, the sacred well spring of life.

Each moment becomes a precious opportunity to honor living from the sacred source of life. Whatever form life comes in, there is an unseen blessing and message of divinity. Surrender to the ease of being with whatever comes, trusting in the innate wisdom of life.

Blessings are the subtle pointers that you receive in the course of daily life. They assist you in remembering your true divine nature. Blessings come from meeting every day people who spark a remembrance of the divine in you. Great blessings come from the eyes of a child and the wisdom of hearts so often over-looked. Blessings come from the tenderness and wisdom of our elders, so often misunderstood and unacknowledged. Blessings come in knowing that your essential nature is love itself, and a sharing of that love and kindness to all that you come across.

YOUR INTENTION IN TRUTH

The intention to live in your truth comes from the recognition of your true nature that is always present, found in the silence of your spiritual heart. As you practice the art of return, you will naturally turn your attention within, realizing all comes from the emptiness and silence of being. The light of intention is to be deeply devoted to the source of your true self. The habit is to be untrue to our source, and follow the outward stream of life into all its entanglements and suffering. The intention to live in your truth will guide you from looking outward, to looking within, to the wisdom of your eternal nature.

The intention to live in the truth of your being must steadfast amongst the changing nature of your visible reality. It then, becomes a daily prayer, living in the art of return to the silence of your being. You will soon become more familiar with your sacred resting place, deepening your communion and understanding of your true nature. Your true self, is a beautiful and radiant being, who abides in the sacred and quiet of the divine. Know that in daily life you are not separated from your true self. Your daily prayer and meditation can be one of bringing your wandering consciousness back to its source, resting in the silence of your spiritual heart.

Each new moment is an opportunity to live in the love and truth of your sacred self. As each new moment arises, surrender all to the healing light of the divine. In each new moment, there is a new breath that brings the awareness back to your true nature of silence. As the art of return becomes your dance of life, you will be continually called back to deepen your rest in the light of your being. This light is the source of all activity, thoughts and actions.

Hold the light of your being in great reverence, knowing that this light is the light of the world. Live in constant recognition that you are this light, the light that makes us one. The ebb and flow of consciousness is to go out of your silence into expression, returning to your eternal pure light of being. This is the foundation for all action that is aligned with your divinity. Holding the light within is to live in the love of your true self, the heart of the divine. Remain in this love no matter what is appears.

Meditation: The Eternal Moment

 The moment is the very breath that you breathe, blessed with infinite possibilities.

The eternal moment is the sacred vitality of life, untouched by the past or projection into the future, timeless and eternal.

The eternal moment is the birth of the new, honoring the sacred grace of life.

The eternal moment is where freedom is found, no bondage, no illusions.

The eternal moment is where your innermost reality is found, a direct perception to the source of all.

The eternal moment is the place of absolute stillness and holy communion.

Everyone is so overridden by thoughts; that's why

they have so much heartache and sorrow. At times I give myself

up to thought purposefully; but when I choose,

I spring up from those under its way.

I am like a high flying bird, and thought is a gnat:

how should a gnat overpower me?

RUMI

CHAPTER SIX

TURNING THE ATTENTION INWARD

❧

Surrender to Your True Nature
Cherish the Temple Within, the sanctuary of the heart
The Source of Your Being
Meditation: The Celestial Light of Oneness

SURRENDER TO YOUR TRUE NATURE

The recognition that there is only pure consciousness in truth, is to surrender to the peace, light and silence of your pure consciousness. Upon surrendering to your sacred essence, all false identification, impressions and accumulated memories are immersed in the light of your true nature. The gateway to this place of unbounded consciousness is the door of your soul, always open and assisting your return. All that is required in divine law is the surrender to that which is always present within, your true eternal self.

Seeing the reality of our identification with the world and the suffering it brings will propel you to shift identity from your personal nature to your impersonal timeless nature. In this shift, you see the futility of holding on to the memories of life's occurrences as being the ultimate reality. Memories, good and bad, are the changing scenery of life, but the background is your true reality. Knowing that the scenery is in constant change, you begin to relate to the vital force of life itself, behind all the changing scenery.

Surrendering into your true nature is to let go of the willful self, meeting the sage within, honoring and cherishing this ancient soul. This sage, who is the dweller within all hearts, is a sacred being with great wisdom and knowing. This vital force is the return of truth in your life, leaving layers of false identity behind.

Surrendering to your true nature, which is in reality the Christ consciousness of all hearts, brings a new life of peace, harmlessness, and a great love for truth. All personal effort is put aside as the divine will within reveals itself and sets the course home to the sacred.

Surrendering is a great and profound turning within, merging your self with divine consciousness. It brings a renewal of being and a new vitality for life, seeing that all parts of your life, which have been devoted to the personal self, have been a mirage. There is an eternal sense of knowing, and freedom from all conditioning as you surrender into the light of pure consciousness. This surrender brings about a great lightness and bliss of being, revealing the peace of your true nature.

A momentous revelation is meeting the true self within, all personal striving is thrown into the sacred fire of truth. Surrendering to your eternal nature, brings a safety never known before, a security that is ever-lasting and protected by infinite grace.

CHERISH THE TEMPLE WITHIN

The body is a temple of God, a temporary vehicle, to be honored and treasured as our greatest opportunity to discover our sacred being. This living ashram is a place of stillness, where you serve that which is holy. By grace, we have been given this vehicle to learn of our true nature, which is pure God consciousness. This vehicle should be cherished as a tool to understand the essence of divinity that is within each human being. Our temple within, is our sacred resting place where we experience our true essence of peace and pure consciousness.

The luminous body is a fragile instrument of spirit and needs much care and honoring of the eternal being, who temporarily inhabits it. Honor this lifetime as a most precious opportunity to live in behalf of the true self. When there is a great identity with the physical and sensual gratification as a means to your happiness, there is again a neglect of the inner life. Treasuring this vehicle is to allow it to rest, to know peace, to know nurturing, and to be free from the burdens of the world. Listening within, your temple will reveal the wisdom necessary to keep it sacred and ready to serve your journey home.

THE SOURCE OF YOUR BEING

You are the sacred embodiment of God's grace, worthy of all manifestations of goodness, love, and great blessings. Upon surrendering to that which lives within, eternal and true, all things of the past are washed from your being, reclaiming your spiritual birthright in this life. This birthright is unimaginable happiness, peace, and contentment. These are the gifts of spirit, given freely, when you turn inside to your ever-abiding true nature.

The light of your radiant being, releases all worldly identification as you turn inward to your path of freedom. Life becomes a series of letting go, until you become turned inside out; all is purified by your inner light. The inner light of your being, reveals the path to service and truth as you deepen your journey. A great divine mystery takes your life on an unplanned journey, as you let go of the known and tread upon the unknown. Living from your source is living in the light of grace, trusting in life to show you the way.

Knowing that all manifestation is subject to change; you remain in constant oneness with the source, unaffected by all that appears. Letting go, opens your life to grace, accepting whatever is revealed and allowing the heart to embrace all that comes. The return to your source of being is to retreat into the silence of the heart, your eternal nature. As you are immersed in the source of divine energy within, there is a complete recognition of eternal self. The master within, reveals the teachings of the universe and becomes your sacred guide in daily life.

Silence brings all that has been divided and fragmented into wholeness, where all becomes one with the sacred source of life. The person that has been known to exist and to carry memory of the past is submerged into the source of your being. When the separate individual dissolves into this great cosmic sea, there is only oneness, in this oneness you are free.

Meditation: The Source of All

 Go into the quiet of your inner being, observing the immense vastness of your silence.

As you deepen your quiet, letting go of all distractions, you will sense the sacred source that is behind all of life.

Your sacred source, will carry you deeper and deeper into the silence of your being. This sacred source is your resting place, the place of infinite stillness.

The infinite stillness of creation is where we meet, where there is only oneness with the source of all.

If you bring forth what is inside of you,

what you bring forth will save you. If you don't bring

forth what is inside of you, what you don't bring forth

will destroy you.

JESUS

CHAPTER SEVEN

THE AWAKENED BEING

🪷

Living with Divine Intelligence
Integrated Awareness
Seeing, Living Life Anew
Meditation: The Heart of Wisdom

LIVING WITH DIVINE INTELLIGENCE

In each human being there is an innate, divine intelligence that is rarely touched. This divine intelligence is the supreme intelligence, untainted by thought, memory, and time, stemming from the universal source of the infinite. The mind, when silent, is unbounded and free to discover the pure consciousness of your being that reflects the divine consciousness of the heavenly world.

The intelligence of your being, when expressed, has the ability to soar to the edges of eternity and to infinite understanding. Intelligence that is unconditioned, free to act according to the truth of being, is one with divine wisdom, the source of life. The awakening process begins when there is a letting go of all identification with anything that bounds you to thoughts, belief, or memory, seeing that your true nature is freedom. When the mind is liberated from the habits of identification, you turn inward to the eternal path of wisdom.

The return to your natural resting-place of silence leads you to surrender all things of a personal nature, into the light of your divine intelligence. The mind is a reflective pool that has the ability to discriminate between thoughts that are geared toward validating the personal self and thoughts that reflect the light of the inner truth. The awakened being, is intelligence in action, observing all that enters in your consciousness, remaining detached and whole in nature.

The awakened being turns to the divine source of silence within to express, the wisdom, love, and divine will of the sacred. In the silence of the mind and heart, you will realize the spaciousness and emptiness of your true nature. As you deepen your understanding of your sacred nature, all conditions that stem from the impermanent, will be released to that which is eternal, and unchanging.

The awakened being sees the nature of the will and how it is directed either to self-pleasure or surrendered to higher good. Through awareness of your true self, you can see when the will is used for self-gain, it plants the seeds of suffering personally and globally. Awareness becomes vigilant to see this will and discern from the personal and the impersonal desires and thought patterns. Awareness is the art of the true self, opening the inner eye of wisdom, seeing all and remaining in emptiness.

Awareness is the skill of quieting your personal inclination to entertain thoughts, emotions, and desires, that are geared to temporary self-gain. Awareness is the supreme understanding of desire and the fruits of desire. The awakened being seeks to stop the roller coaster of pleasure and pain, ending the involvement and belief in a personal story. The awakened being always turns towards its source, the heart of wisdom, the everlasting source of inner strength.

The awakened being quietly listens, trusting in the source of its being and the sacred movement of life. There is a continual awareness of life, seeing it is not about fulfillment of the personal seeker, it is the recognition that you are a free and whole human being. The awakened mind is completely aware of the personal self and how it reappears for recognition and survival, always laying it back to rest in its source of silence.

The awakened being ends the habit of identification with this body and mind, and returns to the source of consciousness. In the depths of stillness, there is only recognition of what is true and eternal within the soul. The most powerful tool that we have as spiritual beings is the ability to see with an awakened intelligent mind and use this seeing as a sword to cut through the false nature of existence. The mind that is silent has the space for great perception of the direct stream of pure consciousness. This pure consciousness is the essence of real love; the eternal source of life.

The awakened being takes the fork to the sacred, clearing any illusion, conditions and patterns that have obscured clear seeing. The awakened one turns within, to the sacred path of the divine, trusting the journey as your eternal home, ever-deepening the awareness of the infinite. Your eternal home, is the silence of your infinite being, your sacred resting-place. It is a place of peace and communion with that which is eternal, vast and unbound.

Your awakened being knows deeply the nature of its source, residing in the sanctuary of your spiritual heart. As the doorway opens to the divine within you, there is an immense amount of energy that floods the soul, washing out any residue of misidentification. Return often to the ever-abiding silence within you, trusting in your eternal divinity found deep within your spiritual heart.

INTEGRATED AWARENESS (THE BLENDING OF THE HEART AND MIND)

Our life is often spent in mistaken identification of who we think we are, believing in the thoughts we think to be real and the emotions that accompany them as our truth. When there is no discernment, between the real and the unreal, the self is carried away into a web of illusion. It is through the integrated awareness of the heart and mind that you can begin the transformation of the self. The loss of the true self can always be traced back to the belief in separation, and from separation thought is born.

When you recognize your true nature without a doubt, all sense of separation is removed in this knowing. There is a firm stance of being, one of knowing that the personal self is non-existent in nature, and you are merely in service to the divine will of life. All is emptied of a personal nature, as the light of your true nature becomes stronger and brighter, leading you to deeper and deeper levels of divine service.

On the path of wisdom, it is possible to develop integrated awareness, seeing with the eyes of love and feeling from the wisdom of truth. It is through the blending of the heart and the mind that creates the full circle of truth. Your true nature is this blending, this integration of love and wisdom. Integrated seeing is to be engaged in the love of your being at all times, accessing the wisdom of your true nature.

The separate self who claims to believe in the thoughts and emotions that come and go is caught in the web of illusion. Your true nature, the divine witness to all, is the master of this separate self. It is your inner truth, the divine self that has the duty of mastering, the belief in a separate ego-self. Integrated awareness is to use the love of your true nature and the wisdom of your higher mind in healing any separation. A great humbling occurs when we can admit we are not the doer in our life. The compassionate heart sees clearly that all must be brought to silence, in this silence, all separation becomes whole.

The most useful tool when you are caught in the illusion of thoughts and emotions, is being steadfast in self inquiry. The inquiring mind is a mind that is devoted and steadfast in finding the truth, leading you to freedom. Integrated awareness is seeing with the totality of being, your divine love and wisdom.

The compassionate heart is the heart of witness consciousness, where all is seen unconditionally, what is observed is brought to the healing light of silence. The wisdom of your true nature sees clearly, without the interference of the ego-self, all is seen in the light of divine witnessing.

The moment is the effortless being of the true self, where you remain in the center of time, not looking ahead, or looking behind. In this moment all is flowing through consciousness, all is consciousness. There is only compassion that is expressed from your true self, and ever-deepening love.

Living, Seeing Life Anew

To live in this eternal moment there must be a letting go of the past, a release of memory that veils you to truth. In breathing deeply, it is possible to look at life from the point of view of the moment, without any desire to change it or to run away from it. Seeing life anew brings a great vitality and spaciousness to attend to what is calling for healing or attention. Whatever is revealed in your consciousness, is coming up for liberation to be set free from identification.

When you are firmly planted in your true nature of witness consciousness, you welcome all that life has to reveal. The recognition that you are not bound by what has passed or what is to come, brings a immense freedom of being. No longer caught in the swing of opposites that are fueled by fear, you remain simply at peace and in observation of whatever comes. Each moment, each day is a new opportunity to affirm the sacred that flows through life, each moment there is a new found freedom of being. In this freedom there is no content to consciousness, only the simple joy of just being.

Living life anew is to bring all areas of life into the beauty of this moment, and to no longer identify with a separate self that is living in the experiences of the past or projection into the future. Each moment is a new miracle of life; your true nature is an unfolding flower, each petal bringing a ever-deepening essence of the divine. Living life anew is to truly be this flower and enjoy the unfolding light of your being.

Living life as if each moment is fresh and alive, not tainted with the past, or anxiously projecting into the future, offers an of ease of being and the possibility to really live in peace. Seeing life anew, and living anew, is applying the love and wisdom of your true nature freely to each moment. Living life anew is to recognize the wholeness of your true self, living each new day from the love and wisdom of your inner truth, with no reference to the past.

Meditation: The Heart of Wisdom

Within the center of your being, you may turn to the heart of wisdom, where your divine essence is found.

Each beat of this heart of wisdom, is pulsating to the divine song, the rhythm of the infinite.

Each new beat is the birth of the new, where you touch into infinite possibilities.

The heart of wisdom is a place of rest and renewal, where you have unlimited access to your sacred vitality.

Your heart of wisdom is a gift from the divine, a sanctuary of peace, love and eternal wisdom. Return to this place often, and listen.

Silence is the best Sadhana...

Nothing like silence to still the waves of restlessness in your

heart... Silence is the speech of the spiritual seeker and the only

language of the realized... He who has reached stillness and

silence, both of which mean the nature of Pure Consciousness,

will enjoy the highest peace and highest bliss.

SRI SATHYA SAI BABA

CHAPTER EIGHT

THE INNOCENCE OF BEING

The Return to Innocence
Peace and Bliss of Being
Living with Insight
Meditation: Trust

THE RETURN TO INNOCENCE

In our human nature, we often spend our life racing to grow up and be in the world. While on the way, we lose our innocence of being and sense of wonderment. At some point, we yearn for the inner child and begin the search for the self that is left behind. The mind races on, projecting into adulthood, with its desires for personal freedom and to "become someone" in life. This conditioning, which is deeply embedded in all of us, takes us further and further away from our truth. At some point in life, we long for the joy of our true nature and we begin the search for the lost sense of self. The growing up and becoming process often leads us to a hardness of being, where the veils block our true nature.

Our lives are spent becoming, searching for the perfect outer circumstances, while deep in our hearts we are longing for a long lost sense of wonderment and happiness. Our search rarely takes us within, as we frantically try to fulfill one passing desire after another. The seeking to fulfill desires stems from this lost sense of self. It is in the return to the inner life that we finally realize that all along it was the light of our being that we have been searching for.

Upon the realization that the self is a divine child within, you rejoice once more in the innocence of being. Your true nature is the untouched part of you that has remained totally innocent and pure throughout all of life's experience. When you recognize the living child within, you will reclaim a sense of wonder and delight in each precious moment. The true self has within its nature the lightness and joy of a child, when the conditioning of thoughts and emotions do not hide it.

It is a divine child-like being that resides in the depth of your heart, revealed when the mind and its changing thoughts and emotions are no longer identified. When there is a gentle acceptance of the simple truth of just being, the most delicate and precious light shines in this acceptance.

The innocence of being is found within the temple of your heart, where the hardness of personal motives and self-attaining energy is left behind. The temple is open to all who shed the outer layer of the worldly self, entering with nothing hidden. The light of your inner-most self, your childlike nature, delights in the joy of life, always living in the moment of unconditional love. Your innermost heart is the heart of a child, full of happiness and pure peace, a heart that is playful and free. Your inner child-like nature lives in the innocence of being.

Peace and Bliss of Being

Your nature is pure bliss and innate happiness, covered by the veil created by misidentification, which occurs when you believe your true reality is found in outward appearances. This outward reality of life is in constant change bringing an array of experiences that swing from pleasure to painful. During all changes, there is the eternal aspect of consciousness that remains in peace, awareness and embedded in divine love. You are this eternal consciousness.

Understanding your true nature, offers great comfort from the changing scenery of life. Notice that throughout time, there is always the part of you that remains unchanged. See how this part is deeply untouched and joyous in nature.

Sorrow occurs when life's difficulties, are taken so seriously believing that this temporary existence is your only reality. All of your sacred energy is given to suffering and the belief in the temporary story of life. Turn your sacred energy within and retreat to the wellspring of your being where you receive the nurturing needed from the eternal source of peace. The peacefulness, which is your true abiding nature, is always present within for your renewal of spirit.

Life is a complicated journey, when so many conditions and requirements are projected for happiness and contentment. This often leaves little room for peace. You must stop the projection of the self and turn the attention inward to the source of all fulfillment. You see clearly that chasing after desires for personal happiness is never a means to an end. There is not the cessation of desire because nothing can satisfy the empty nature of the personal self.

There is only peace and bliss in your true nature, when all ideas of separation end. When you turn within, the great fire of truth ignites to burn away the false identity that has accumulated from the belief in a personal self, with its deep conditioning of memory and time. Peace and bliss are left when this inner fire burns the veils of separation that have been created to living in your true reality, your divine pure consciousness.

In knowing your true nature, you can return home at any time to experience the nurturing of the peace and quiet that is always present within you. The beauty of life is that in each new moment there is a new opportunity for this return.

"Trust in yourself" that you are the happiness you seek and that under the personal identification with the temporary nature of life, you are an eternal being an embodiment of peace and bliss, always present in silence.

LIVING IN INSIGHT

The moment between each breath there is a vastness and emptiness so profound that it brings you into direct contact with the source of creation, grace itself. Breathe deeply and allow your true nature to reveal itself, in the silence of your being.

Your true nature, the master within, calls back the wandering habits of the personal self, into the healing light of silence. Insight into your true nature continually deepens, as you remain in the quietness of your being, where the wisdom of the universe is revealed.

Communion with your own divinity is the natural blessing that is born from the silence of your being. Insight into your beingness is pure grace, as the veils of illusion are lifted up gently, uncovering your radiance. Ever-deepening, you will discover more and more luminosity, as you let go and see what is revealed. This letting go brings you to a deeper level of recognition and understanding of your God-Self. You are a fragment in the life of God and extraordinary beauty will be revealed to you as you deepen your insight into your eternal reality. Your insight is the opening of your wisdom eye, where the noises of the temporary nature of life is silenced. Your inner vision, opens you to the unknown where you embark upon a path, to the infinite, mysterious universe.

The wisdom of your true nature is veiled by the illusion of a separate consciousness, that believes in the appearances of life as the only reality.

Deep in your knowing, there is the wisdom of the self, directly connected to God's infinite wisdom. Trust in that knowing, seeing that this world is a temporary stopover, full of illusions and false security. Insight is having the discernment to see the real from the unreal and to choose wisely in this lifetime.

With insight into your true reality, you will live in the light of the eternal, walking the path of your truth. Your divine path will lead to all the wisdom and insight needed for your journey. As you return to your true self, resting in your awareness, the light in your true nature will guide you on your path. Know now that the gifts of the spirit are yours to partake of. By returning to your divine source, you can **"Trust in Yourself."**

Meditation: Trust

Retreat within to your ever-abiding true nature, where you may trust the wisdom and guidance of the living sage with your being.

Your true nature is effortless, where all striving, attaining or becoming may be put aside

Relax deep within, knowing that this is the rest that nourishes your inner spirit, opening to your divine reality.

When you meet your true self, all fears, concerns, worries are drowned in the light of this meeting.

Trust is living in your divine reality, in complete surrender.

The light which shines in the eye is really the light of the heart.

The light which fills the heart is the light of God,

which is pure and separate from the light

of intellect and sense.

RUMI

CHAPTER NINE

IDENTIFICATION WITH THE REAL

Courage, the Inner Strength to See
Living the Truth of Yourself
Mistaken Identity
Meditation: Living in Fullness

COURAGE, THE INNER STRENGTH TO SEE

To live in a world where there is great suffering and negativity requires great courage. Living with courage is holding the intention to be free from needless personal sorrow and to no longer contribute to the sorrow of humanity. Each moment is new opportunity to reflect upon your life, accessing the courage needed from your inner truth. The courage to see, requires observation with honesty and integrity; the workings of the personal self. The courageous soul sees the impermanent nature of things, turning within to rest in the eternal source of life.

Returning to the light of your being will nurture and reveal the truth of your self, giving you more and more strength to live in your light. Retreating to this place of stillness within, requires courage and trust in yourself, knowing this is your true home. Courage to see the false in life must be there in order to see the real, lasting, and unchanging nature of things.

Most people spend their lives chasing after a desire and rejecting that which is no longer wanted. It is like being locked up in a maze, going around in circles, never finding the center. The divine center within cannot be found in the pursuit of self-gratification. It is only found in spiritual heart, free from identification with the personal self.

To live for the truth of the moment takes great courage. The tendency is to have a reference point from memory. When living in each eternal moment, you must have the courage to allow the new to transpire by releasing the past. To live with courage, is to be a warrior of the true self. This requires you to observe the workings of thought and desire in life. Courage and love go hand in hand as these qualities assist you in remaining ever mindful and compassionate to the workings of the ego-self. Observing the nature of the mind to identify with the outward stream of life, takes great courage. In this observation, you return to silence of being, where all separation is immersed in the light of oneness.

It is important to remember to have courage when it comes to really looking at the false. Conditioning, past experiences, and misguided ways can be frightful when they come up for view. The more fear, the greater identification is with a personal self, believing in a personal experience that is rooted in time and memory. Until the true self is realized, there is often an unquestionable belief in life of the individual, with all its memories and stories. The bravery of the soul comes from being clear that you are not your past, your body, or your memories. Your participation in life's drama came from the mistaken identity that you have taken yourself to be.

Compassionate and loving attention to the self and surrender to what is true, will make the transition from the temporary to the eternal. Observation is the act of being courageous. Letting go of all that is false will bring about a freedom, a breath of fresh air to your being. This observation of yourself should be a gentle one of non-judgment and should elicit total acceptance as to what is seen. Courage is seeing things the way they are, discerning the real from the unreal, and uncovering the essence of your true nature.

LIVING THE TRUTH OF YOURSELF

In your truest reality, you are a spark of the divine. As you realize your true nature, you will recognize that you are a whole human being, not fragmented by time, or life's experience. Your true reality is timeless and remains the same throughout all experiences in the changing nature of life. Your true nature, a being of light, has chosen a body for the purpose of self-realization.

Awareness of your eternal nature deepens, as you surrender into the silence of your sacred presence.

Each moment is an opportunity to see the wholeness and unity of your being. As you uncover your wholeness, the truth of your being, you will no longer live in the fragments of the personal self. All fragments of the personal self will become unified with your tue nature.

Living in your truth is to reside in your spiritual heart, always being true to your sacred nature. Your true self is the light that is guiding you home to your sacred resting place. As you touch into the light, accessing your unlimited being, the direct source of divine wisdom is experienced. This wisdom is your essential nature, realized in your deepest silence. Silence itself is the vehicle to reach this true source of wisdom, as within each being there is a direct contact with the Divine.

Your own individuality merges with the infinite, when there is complete surrender of separation. There is a new found wisdom, seeing all as stemming from the great oneness of life. In this oneness, you see that in truth, all is consciousness, and you are infinitely apart of the whole. The letting go of all separation brings you into the light of the divine where the universe is a great circle of divine energy. Allow the divine being within you to guide you to live a life that is true to your sacred source.

Your true reality, your divine nature, is never affected by the ever-changing nature of the world. A lifetime of sorrow, pleasure, and pain can be viewed from much more detachment when you know your true reality. You are an eternal being, untouched by all of life's manifestation, Trust in Yourself, resting deeply in your truth.

MISTAKEN IDENTITY

The moment there is a meeting with your eternal true nature, the ending of worldly identification occurs, and the realization happens that you are one with the cosmic flow of life. All sense of separation dissolves in this oneness, the spark of your divinity now shines. At which time, there is the transition from identification with the outer temporary reality to your inner eternal reality, a great light is revealed that assists your return to your true nature. The divine presence within appears and there is a feeling that you no longer walk this path alone.

When the identity shifts from the separate ego-self to the true self, all of your being comes into holiness or wholeness. When you stop the identification with the "doer" of your life, then the miracle of life occurs. Life then works through your being and there is not the illusion of a separate individual in control.

Life is an expression of the divine, where all things stem from silence, when you surrender control. Observe, how your life unfolds when you are not directing it. Action stems from the truth of the moment, originating from the awareness of your true nature. This is the point when the seeds of the personal self are no longer being planted in the garden of illusion, resulting in unnecessary suffering.

In the light of pure consciousness, all is an expression of the universal source of sacred energy, happening beyond personal effort or control. In this way, all expressions reflect the love and truth of your being. Your true destiny is to know yourself as an embodiment of pure love and pure wisdom. The love and wisdom of your true nature, has immense freedom when there is no longer the identification with a separate individual. Freedom is your true nature, discovered when there is no longer the belief in personal nature as your reality, freedom is found in the unbounded consciousness that you are.

Meditation: You are Truth

Uncover your radiance, letting go the hardness of personal identity, allowing the beauty that you are to shine through.

In your radiance, your true nature, ever deepens to the pure love, light and truth of the divine.

In the sacred stillness of your being, rest deeply, it is in this stillness that the truth of your being is revealed.

Perhaps you may come upon

that mystery which nobody can reveal

to you and nothing can destroy

KRISHNAMURTI

CHAPTER TEN

THE ART OF LIVING

Sadhana, the Art of Living
Service, Responsibility
Service, Divine Love
Meditation: Living in Fullness

SADHANA, THE ART OF LIVING

It is important to learn how to live skillfully so that the charms, temptations, and attractions of the world do not create obstacles to living in your true self. Everything in the phenomenal world is subject to change, so it is very important to practice non-attachment. The external world moves in cycles of opposites, the nature of creation. Our salvation from the pairs of opposites is to live in the eternal where all is one, embraced in love. Living in your true eternal nature is simply being unaffected by the cyclic nature of change, staying in witness consciousness, turning toward the eternal flow of life as your true reality. The nature of your true reality is emptiness and spaciousness of being, where you can remain at peace amidst the ever-changing nature of life.

There are two laws that can be noticed in daily life, the law of expansion and the law of contraction. When you become a victim of the little mind and suffer from destructive emotions and the belief in passing thoughts, contraction occurs. Contraction is the result of the deep-seated fear in the person who believes whole-heartedly in their personal thoughts and emotions, resulting in living a life where you are in constant reaction. You may find yourself always trying to create happiness from the outer realm or running away from the part of life with which you are not happy. This is the cycle of the mind that looks to external reality for happiness and peace. Ending the habit of this outward looking and retreating to your inner eternal nature is the path to everlasting happiness and peace.

The law of expansion is seeing the impermanence of life's passing drama and expanding your consciousness into eternal consciousness, into the ever-deepening state of pure love and acceptance. Expanding is to use whatever comes about in life as a pointer to move to higher levels of awareness and love. Expansion of your being, while life is falling apart, is a constant reminder of what lives eternally within, and accepting and allowing life's outer changes. It is through the falling apart of what is no longer working, that gives spaciousness for the new to come. The grace of life is always assisting you to let go and surrender deeper and deeper into your limitless and eternal nature.

Surrendering to your true self is to withdraw from the stimulation and distraction of the senses, seeing that you are whole and complete without any indulgence at all. Withdrawal of the senses from outward desires is very important in tapping your eternal nature. The mind, when centered in divinity, comes to rest in the silence and peace of its true nature. The peace of your true nature will see all in the light of truth and grace. Trust in your peace within, where you can offer all disturbances to this healing light.

The true work of the soul is to retreat deeply into the flow of divine energy within, deeply witnessing all passing phenomena, remaining untouched and free from appearances. The sacred essence within you will guide you to transcend the will of the personal self to the will of the Divine.

The desire to know your inner-most truth, the yearning to live a life free from personal suffering, is the fuel that you need to light the flame of your heart. The path to your true self is well illuminated, as you turn your personal will to the will of the divine. Offer your daily prayer to the sacred within, living in the light of your true nature where you are inherently free and abundant with love, truth, wisdom and peace.

SERVICE, RESPONSE-ABILITY

Service is acting according to the dictates of your heart and responding in the moment, free from a personal motive. Being in the moment, free from entanglements of the past, is holding the intention for service. Awareness is born from the love of your true nature, service is applying this love to whatever life presents. Service is simply living in your truth, shining the light of your true nature.

Early in life we are guided to live by the conditioning of our personal self. We are deeply conditioned to live according to the values of a broken world that is ill from seeking personal gratification. Service begins with the compassionate heart, seeing the truth of life and acting with integrity, honoring the sacred in life. Service is removing the illness of separation in our life, bringing ourselves back to the wholeness of our true nature. Service is having unlimited compassion for this journey while loving your inner being, seeing through the veils, accumulated through our selfhood.

True service is when there is an understanding of wholeness, knowing that each fragment is essential to the whole. In this understanding you feel a deep responsibility to find wholeness within, to assist the healing of all of humanity.

Response-ability is the action of responding in the moment to the teaching of life. When responding in the moment, you are free from the past. In this freedom it is possible to serve and unconditionally apply the love that is required for life. We are very graced to have the ability to live a life in service to pure consciousness, to live according to the dictates of our true selves. The true grace of divinity is when we see the cause of suffering, turning our life inward to what is everlasting and eternal. The radical change in consciousness is when our attention turns away from the personal nature of life, toward the sacred. This change deepens our compassion and love for the sacred in life, leading you to live a life beyond the personal.

This is the greatest work of life, to become free from personal bondage and suffering, knowing that in this freedom you are truly assisting the healing process of the human condition. Your true destiny is to know yourself as an embodiment of pure love, reflecting this love in all areas of your life. Love is attention to all things lacking in the moment. You are holding a golden chalice of love, ready to give to all. This is the true meaning of service. Knowledge of your true self, love of yourself, and love of others, is the pathway to becoming a whole human being.

SERVICE OF DIVINE LOVE

One of the greatest services you can give to others is that of seeing others as your true self. As you see yourself in the light of pure consciousness, you will also see others in the same light. Seeing the good in people and knowing they are pure God-consciousness is a way of assisting them to know their true selves. This seeing is the very act of love. In seeing the truth in yourself and in all beings, a letting go of the false occurs. What remains is the pure beauty of the Divine. Life has blessed each and every human with a span of time to practice the art "knowing thyself."

This time is so very precious and its a beautiful moment when a soul sees the true meaning of this birth. Life with the purpose of uncovering the veils to truth, is a life that goes beyond personal suffering. Suffering is a fact of life, but when viewed in the light of your true nature, you are able to live with less attachment to the impermanent nature of life. There is an ever-deepening understanding of life, and the nature of the self who is the creator of sorrow, through misidentification. Suffering is viewed in a much different light when there is the radical understanding that the self who creates sorrows, doesn't truly exist. Through turning inward to meet your sacred eternal being, the personal self will no longer have a voice that stands by itself. You will undeniably, know who you truly are, and the outer life will be changed forever more.

Divine service is living in devotion to your ever-lasting true nature. Sit at the feet of your own inner master in great devotion to the sacred within your being, this is your path to joy and peace. Service to the Divine is an act of selflessness, a time of remembrance, and a great humility that opens you to the communion with your own Christ light. Service is opening your inner lotus in love and devotion to the source of all life. A great service to all is to Trust in

Yourself, where you see you are the light of the world. As the light of each being grows stronger, the world becomes brighter.

Meditation: Living in Fullness

The fullness that is away present awaits you, in the stillness of your heart.

A simple letting go of the thoughts, concepts, and conditioning that have been born through worldly identification is all that is needed to return to the fullness of your true nature.

Breathing in, just allow the fullness of your radiant being to be present. In this divine presence, there is nothing lacking.

You are the abundance of the sacred vitality of life itself, in your fullness you are pure beauty, grace, and the embodiment of joy

An inner effort must always be undertaken in a deep state of sur-

render, in order to create a space within the person to receive the

flow of higher energy. While the nature of surrender is essentially

open and passive, the process of energy absorption is active.

BERNADETTE ROBERTS

CHAPTER ELEVEN

SURRENDER

The Art of Surrender
Letting Go, Generosity of Being
All Things Change
Meditation: Surrender

THE ART OF SURRENDER

Surrender is the complete giving up of your personal striving, with the deep understanding that in truth, you are not a separate individual who strives, attains or becomes something. This is the sincere recognition that you already are a full human being, whose identity is found through turning toward your true self. Deep inside your true nature lives a divine being, whole, true and not dependent on the outside whatsoever. In surrendering unto that, there is a letting go to the sacred force that operates your life. In a sense, it is the art of giving, for in true surrender, you must give yourself to the sacredness of yourself.

Surrender is complete trust in that which is and always has been, whole, true, and eternal. Surrender is to release your personal hold on the passing nature of life, allowing the mystery of life's movement to take your being down the river of grace.

The alleviation of personal suffering is to let go of all accumulated memories and identification with impermanence. This action of letting go and surrendering often triggers great fear of losing your known identification. Our true destiny which is the recognition that we are eternal and one with all of life is to see now the truth of our being. The separate identity that we take ourselves to be is just a wave in the ocean eternity. When the wave is only aware of itself, the wave experiences separation. When the wave dissolves all sense of separateness, it no longer holds anything apart from this ocean. Surrendering is the recognition that you are not a separate wave with all the distinctions of separation.

The will, when directed to your divinity, will assist you in the return to your eternal nature. The will, when directed to self-gratification, will only bring you the fruits of your temporary desires. Surrendering your will to the Divine assists the natural flow of life. The great beauty is that all of your being can be an extension of divine will, surrendering to the greater movement of life.

Surrendering the personal will is to put aside the strong identification with the 'I' thought, realizing the untruth of this constant pursuit. It is reclaiming your inner divinity of peace and contentment, where there is a natural ease of being. Your inner divinity is held by a sacred thread connecting you to the source of creation, where the infinite is ever-unfolding in its magnificence.

Surrendering is the divine work of all souls, no longer believing in the personal will to guide you through life. This is seen deeply when you turn to divine will of silence, where the wisdom of your inner truth speaks without the condition of a personal motive or self-gain. When there is an understanding of your timelessness, a vigilance appears to see the truth of the personal self, and its activity of reaping of pleasure and pain. Most of life we spend vacillating between pleasure and pain, due to our desires, and eventually we begin to see that it has its roots in the personal will. To surrender to your true nature is to retreat into the silence of your being and see that all truth comes from this silence and awareness. Your true nature, is pure awareness; an abundance of divine insight and discernment. When you live from your innate awareness, you are free from the web of the personal will. This freedom is where the key to your eternal wisdom is found.

Surrendering to the silence of your being will open the inner doors to reality, where the infinite is found. Live your life in prayer with your sacred nature, releasing the past, breathing in the new, and allowing space for life to unfold. Life, the most precious movement, has space to reveal its great beauty, love, forgiveness, and compassion in this surrender.

LETTING GO, THE GENEROSITY OF BEING

Letting go to all things that are not in direct reality with your true nature of divinity, is the most sacred process in uncovering what is vital and eternal. The art of letting go, is to first see clearly that your true nature, is revealed only in freedom where you hold no past. In letting go and dying to the past, we learn to truly live in the moment, giving our self to life instead of demanding from it.

Our inner work is to remain current, always new in relationship to life's movement. The moment is full of life's teaching, opening and unfolding to the truth of being. Letting go is the art of giving to life, the supreme generosity of being, where you live in communion with the sacred. Letting go is to release any personal holdings that prevent you from living in your true nature. In generosity of being, you live in a state of gratitude finding ways to serve this life. In the light of your true nature there is no longer a holding onto that which serves the small self, there is a giving up of the old, and a willingness to serve in any way that life presents itself. Letting go is to find yourself floating in the current of life, amazingly natural and honoring the moment, walking in the light of divine will.

In letting go, we must see clearly how our moments are spent with conditioned response from the past. This is the very root of why the new can never be experienced. The love of your being is yearning to just be, without any contamination from past experiences. Generosity of being is to give up, give of yourself to the moment, and give all that is holding the self from fully living now.

Letting go is dying to our patterns, our habits of believing in our separate individual self. It is to see clearly without a doubt that our true nature is beyond any limitation of self-identity and that we are a spark of greatness. This greatness is not from the light of a small self, it is in the light of the infinite of which we are apart. All our small, individual thinking is blown away by the wind of the most powerful force of the infinite, leaving the silence of the self. In this silence, nothing can be found, but the sound of the universe, the sound of the inner-most heart.

If you were to truly look now in this moment for a personal self, without memories, or past conditioning it would be no where to be found. When there is a letting go of thought about the self, grace will surprise you and the sacred self emerges, out of the quiet and silence of being.

Letting go and living in the moment frees you from past tendencies and conditioning that have bounded you, your family, and your ancestors to the illusion of separation. To be truly free, you must be ever-present, letting go and allowing for the new and eternal possibilities of life. In order to dance with the new, you must die to the old, releasing memories that veil the true self. Through this unveiling, there is a revealing of your sacred nature.

Letting go, is the art of dying to the past, turning toward your true heart to find the gift of life. In your sacred heart, the understanding comes that each moment is holy and offers a renewal of life, where all forgiven, and there is only love.

All Things Change

The nature of life is change, all things in life are subject to the conditions of birth, death, and continual change, manifesting the cycles of nature. Pure consciousness of being, is witness to this change, allowing all to pass through. When we see how conditions in our life are constantly changing, our thoughts, our emotions, and outward circumstances, what remains steadfast and in observation is our witness consciousness. This witness consciousness is the truth of your self, your ever-lasting, luminous being.

Suffering is the result of our unquestionable identification with this changing reality, and the belief that there is separate individual who is in the center of these changes. When we are deeply identified with this reality, thinking that it is permanent, and that there is a person who is acquiring, succeeding, becoming something, the nature of change can be very frightful. There is a great fear of loss, the loss of one's money, acquired objects, health, sexuality, and so on. This fear that most people live with is almost never questioned and investigated.

The heart that carries the burdens and scars of the personal self, is aching to become free from personal sorrow. The heart of wisdom within all beings, is gifted with the ability to discern truth from untruth and the real from the unreal. When the memories of past trauma are released from the heart, it then can open to its potential of great love and healing of all separation. The heart is free from all impressions when there is a realization of the sacred self within, allowing all false identification to be released.

Upon investigation into your true nature, you can access the inner wisdom needed to discern the real from the unreal, and change the thought patterns held in ignorance. See thoughts that are deeply identified with the unreal, transitory condition of life, are thoughts that dissipate when observed in silence. In observing from your true nature, witness consciousness, all that is untrue will just float by, there will no longer be energy given to that which is false in nature.

Deep within the heart, there is the most medicinal source of healing waiting for you, the healing of the misidentification of the human condition. The wisdom of your true nature is readily accessible, as you stop believing in passing thoughts, and there accompanying emotions. It is from the silence of the heart that you meet your greatest teacher, your guide along the path of the self. The light within transforms all fear into love and identification with the impermanent to the eternal, this light is your true home of peace, forever in stillness.

Meditation: Surrender

 Deep inside the quiet of your heart you will find the peace of your being, where you meet your eternal self.

Enter this place leaving all worldly concerns behind, come to your sacred resting place where you will be renewed in spirit.

Letting go of all burdens that this life has challenged you with, know that within the quiet of your heart all is surrendered.

Your sanctuary is always available to you, where you surrender to the quiet within, this your true home of eternal peace.

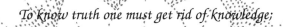

To know truth one must get rid of knowledge;

nothing is more powerful and creative

than emptiness.

LAO-TZU

CHAPTER TWELVE

LIVING IN BALANCE

Living in Balance
Living with Discernment
The Divine Center Within
Meditation: Your Divine Center

LIVING IN BALANCE

Life is an interplay between the divine energies within, and the outward personality, consisting of the body, mind and emotions. The veils to your true nature which are the bodies sensations, your emotional states and the thinker and the thoughts, are quiet powerful in creating the illusion of a separate individual. This is the test of your being, to see through these veils and turn within to find a balance, walking in the light of the sacred. Your true nature is not subject to duality, the process of birth and death, or of time. You are the embodiment of the eternal sacred energy of life, the essence of pure consciousness. Your sacred nature is rarely nurtured and upheld in a lifetime, as daily life is devoted to the outward pursuit of life. Your true nature is always present, in silence, and is infused by the sacred energy of life. Living in balance is to return to your true self, experiencing your divine and eternal nature, unaffected by the chatter of the ego-self.

In the quiet of your spiritual heart, you meet your innermost teacher, who will assist you in uncovering the truth of your being. The understanding of your truth comes from knowing what you are not — your body, your emotions, or your thoughts. This revelation takes you deeper and deeper within until you meet the emptiness of the self, which is pure peace. Upon recognition that you are this peace, the false layers of identification begin to fall away.

Living in balance is to walk in the outer world of manifestation while all along being firmly planted on the inner path to the infinite. This state of equilibrium is found within through effortless being, steadfastly knowing that your true reality is not found in this temporary manifestation. The ease of being that comes from letting go of personal effort, occurs when we flow with the natural unfolding of life.

Living in balance is to understand the root cause of duality, seeing that where there is pleasure, then comes pain. This is the cycle most humans suffer from, and so true happiness and joy that is not based on outward stimulation, is rarely found. When you investigate the nature of the personal self, an awareness develops of the root cause of suffering. You see clearly that a life in pursuit of self-gain is laced with personal suffering. When the nature of the true self is known, which is silence and peace of being, you can easily let go of the struggle of the conditioned mind. This profound change of being is when there is an understanding of the functioning of the body and mind, and that all expressions come from the silence of your true nature. This change leads you to let go of the personal quest for self-pleasure, seeing that it is a never ending road.

The nature of life, being change, is always moving through the cycles of polarities that have to do with the impermanent nature of things. Walking the middle path is to stay centered in your divinity, keenly aware of the polarities in life. When you remain in your truth, you are pure awareness, keeping the channel of your being clear. In this way the love of your being flows purely and there is not a personal self who is swinging through the cycles of desire. Your divine center within is ever-present, the place within you where the you touch the creative spring of life. When you experience the stillness of your true nature, holding the energy within as deeply sacred, you will live your life from the center of your being. Living in balance is to return to the quiet of your being, where there is no personal effort and striving. In constant remembrance of your true nature within, you walk in your divine center, where all expressions come from the emptiness and silence of being.

Compassion for this walk is deeply required, as the nature of manifestation is imperfection, and we are profoundly subject to this condition. The humbling of life

is that you just accept the cyclic nature of appearances, knowing that all manifestation is in a state of change. You see that there is nobody in control and there
is not a doer. Grace is born from this recognition of emptiness, where all efforts
of the personal self are surrendered. Within the silence of your being you are able
to find complete rest and equanimity of being, you see that all of life is created
from the miracle of silence. Living in Balance is to observe the oneness of life,
treating all as sacred, giving it your complete love, and attention in the moment.

Seek within your heart the guidelines for your life, know that all wisdom is
found in your spiritual heart. Upon living the truth of your heart, all expressions of life will be in honor of that. In your true reality you are pure goodness
and wisdom, this is revealed with the personal nature of the self is laid to rest.
Upon, living from your true reality you walk in the silence of your being. Your
true reality is peace itself found when you find the inner balance between the
divine and outward reality, resting in the heart of silence.

LIVING WITH DISCERNMENT

To discern is to see the real from the unreal, in this powerful illusionary stage
we have taken a role on. Living in discernment is remain in your true nature
at all times, with the light of observation. Upon the realization of the true self,
the skill of discernment becomes stronger, seeing all as flowing through consciousness, while remaining in devotion to your sacred nature. The nature of
witness consciousness is divinity, all that displays in this consciousness is
flooded in silence, the truth of your being.

Insight into your inner truth, the wisdom of your soul, becomes accessible as
you retreat in silence. The mind when quiet is a reflection of the source of the
true self, which the pure consciousness of divinity. All things that come into
your life can be viewed in the calmness and peace of your true self. This stillness of the mind is the inner door of wisdom, allowing you to live in complete
harmony with your true nature.

Discernment comes from your inner wisdom, with the strong intention to live according to the voice of your true nature. The mind in its conditioned state, unharnessed by the truth, will continue to spiral down the road of personal suffering. The mind when freed from the conditions of a separate individual, will serve the intention of truth. Living in Discernment requires a great strength of being, to see what is real and what is false, in the display of consciousness. When the mind identifies with itself and the external world, the veil of illusion is created. Your true nature of freedom is revealed as the veil of the personal self falls away.

THE DIVINE CENTER WITHIN

The awakened one lives in the divine center within, treading the path of neutrality and emptiness. The divine center within opens the wisdom eye, the expression of your truth, and the understanding of the heart.

Remaining in the divine center within, is walking the razors' edge of life, in constant remembrance of the truth of your being, seeing the delicate balance of each moment. The divine center is the sacred channel of higher energies, where all identification with the personal ends. It is the place of ebb and flow of consciousness, where you receive the nourishment required to live a life of physical manifestation, while knowing your true source is the eternal. The divine center within the temple of your heart is where you will find the most sacred companion, the presence of the divine.

Live your life from your divine channel, using this sacred energy wisely. As you become more aware of your sacred energy you will see that the personal self and this manifested world is imperfect and a part of the ever changing nature of life. As you learn this, all of life will be seen as sacred, fragile and temporary.

Upon turning within to your divine center you will know that you are at home, regardless in the world of imperfection and constant change. The divine channel within is the direct flow of the sacred energy of life, where there is only emptiness of being. In this emptiness, the eternal is found and you forever walk with the creator.

Meditation: Your Divine Center

 Walking the tightrope of life is simple when you close your eyes to outside distractions.

You simply walk, trusting in each step, allowing the rope, the wind and the force of gravity to guide you.

The divine center within will illuminate your walk creating an inner strength to tread the tightrope of life.

When you walk within you will be a peace, knowing you are supported by the sacred force of life, all distractions are stilled by the radiance of your being.

Return to your inner divine center when the pulls of outward life have exhausted your vitality, this is your refuge.

Always know that your Divine Center within is holding a place for you to rest and let go into the oneness of life.

His thought is quiet,

quiet are his word and deed,

when he has obtained freedom

by true knowledge,

when he has thus become

a quiet man

BUDDHA

CHAPTER THIRTEEN

LIVING IN SILENCE

Attention in Relationship to Silence
Silence, the Fertile Ground of Being
The Illusion of the Personal Self
Meditation: On Emptiness

ATTENTION IN RELATIONSHIP TO SILENCE

Attention is vital to beingness, for when you are not fully in the moment, attention based on truth is impossible. When the personal nature of life is no longer believed to be your true reality, all memory and conditions of separation fall away. What is left is pure beingness, where attention is pure vitality. Silence is the foundation for beingness, it is your sacred resting place, where your radiance shines. The silence of your being is your true nature, immediately accessible by turning your attention away from outer identification.

When attention is turned from outer identification to inner truth, a great strength is applied to all areas of life. Because attention is no longer given to what is untrue, our separate identity, we have immense vitality to uncover what is true. We live our lives from a different point of view, one of seeing without a personal hold onto what is seen. All actions stem from the quiet of our true self, reflecting integrity of being. Integrity of being is to live from the wholeness of your true nature, fully engaged in life with your truth. When you live from your truth, the expression of your sacred being, all action is correct and based on universal wisdom. Right action that is based on the sacred is the action that makes all one, taking responsibility for the whole and living according to this truth.

When attention is applied to the truth of being, a most profound realization occurs of the light of our true nature which is the light of the divine. Attention is the fuel for the truth, for in applying attention in the investigation of your true nature, the false is burned by the light of this attention. Attention is the giving back to life, the generosity of being that is called for from the divine. It is the tool to clear away what is false, and the courage to walk ahead in truth, conviction and steadfastness. A life lived that is alive with attention to your inner true nature, is a life that is free from entanglements of a personal nature. Living in attention is to fully embrace all in the light of truth, knowing that attention is the flame that burns away the unreal.

Living a life of clear attention, is to be in constant communion with the eternal fire of truth, throwing all that is untrue into this fire. Attention to the moment is the instrument of awareness, based on truth, where personal reactions have no voice. The fire of attention is born from complete freedom from the past, applying the sacred energy of the moment, fully without impediment.

The silence within has an immense intelligence, when it is free from the conditions of the personal self. You must learn to yield, bend and heed to this silence, by constantly surrendering your personal investment in each new moment. The sacred silence of our true nature is the voice of attention, when there is no distraction of a personal nature. It is having the freedom to attend to life in whatever way life calls for, this is the true meaning of service.

Living in attention, is to live in the center of being where you can access the vital energy needed to attend to the moment. Remaining in equanimity toward life is to live in the center of all manifestation, not being lead astray by one side of polarity or the other. This point between duality is where the sacred is found, the eternal wellspring of joy and the source of unlimited vital force.

When you touch into the radical freedom of your being, all of the past is wiped away, and you have no reference as to who you are as an individual separate identity. The personal nature of the self with a story, drowns in the flood of divine pure consciousness as you realize your true self. There is no longer a separate individual who identifies with the outer cycles of life. There is a constant awareness of change, embracing the wind of change, flowing with the ebb and flow of this mysterious reality.

Action, when you are free from the personal conditioning and memory has the force of attention needed to uphold your truth throughout all of life's challenges. This action is pure and free from the content of the past. Attention from the silence of being, is when there is complete giving of yourself to the fact of life, the highest love that is accessible to your being.

Know deeply that you are free from all outer conditions, from all things in the past, and in reality that which lives within cannot be touched by any outer circumstance, or affected by time. Through knowing your true self, deeply letting go all coverings of your inner being, you are able to access immense energy for life.

The sacred energy that flows through your being, assists in the opening of your inner self to the depth of understanding. When the inner self is free from identification with the individual ego-self, there is a great fire of attention, being able to discern the real from the unreal. Your true nature is freedom itself, inviting you to partake of the flight of your soul, flowing in the current of your life, peaceful, blissful and one with eternity.

SILENCE, THE FERTILE GROUND OF BEING

Listen quietly within where it is possible to perceive, the emptiness of this vast universe, knowing that all of creation appears from immaculate stillness. Behind all that lives, is the quiet pulse of the sacred, mysterious life force. So still is our true nature, we only need to go to the quiet, to hear its divine melody. The divine music that assists the waves, creating the wind, opening the bud of a rose, all of this comes from the sacred force of the quiet.

In the quiet temple within, we are pure being-ness, free to expand into the vast eternal emptiness from which we come. Silence is a great force that assists in healing our bodies, our minds and emotions, for it is within the silence that all things come into order. Silence is a great expression of order, bringing things into rest, allowing the natural process of balance to take place.

Silence is the storehouse for miracles, as miracles are the blossoms of silence. Looking through the eyes of gratitude, you will begin to observe the truth of life, which is miraculous beyond our comprehension. All gifts of the spirit are discovered in silent observation. The gifts of gratitude, beauty, love, peace, generosity, service; are found in your inner self, born of silence.

Listening to the will of the quiet is to truly listen to your innermost heart, the sacred chalice of love. The silent mind is a mind that is free to perceive the most profound truth. In this perception, the mind is quiet, reflecting the eternal consciousness of omnipresent force of the world.

Through silence it is possible to meet the true being who resides within your heart, opening to the voice of wisdom that speaks from there. It is only through the belief in our separate individual selves that the past is held onto, where there is a constant search for the self, in time and memory. Understanding your true nature is to see that all things from the past and all things in the future are absorbed in the sacredness of true being. In the light of pure consciousness, there is no past or future, for your true eternal nature is found only in the now. In truth you are a whole human being, eternal and untouched by all experience. In silence, all activity of searching comes to an end, for deep in this ocean of infinite truth, the true being that you are is realized.

Daily life is full of challenges, offering many opportunities to observe the world of change, seeing the cause and effect of pleasure and pain. Each day is a new display of this change, the challenge is to remain mindful of your eternal nature. The life of the disciple of truth is to turn away from believing in this changing unreality, surrendering each moment to the divine truth of the infinite. Being in the world, functioning and living according to your truth, is the expression of your true self, that lives in the luminosity of your heart.

From the fertile ground of silence springs forth the nature of the divine, with incredible beauty, joy, untold happiness and peace of mind. All expressions of truth come from this silence of being, the ever-unfolding mystery of life.

THE ILLUSION OF THE PERSONAL SELF

The belief that there is an individual who lives life fulfilling their identity through the world, is the ground for all suffering. The illusion of the personal self becomes known when you see how this self has lead you into countless years of personal suffering. Upon looking, you will never find a personal self who attains anything, what is found is only in the context of thought and memory. When there is a letting go of the thought of who you think you are from the past, or what you will be in the future, you are only left with the emptiness of being. When you turn within to the silence of the true self, there is the understanding that all images, and concepts of yourself are born from thought. Through silence you will reveal the emptiness of your being where you hold the mystery of pure and divine consciousness

When the illusion of your apparent reality, is seen in the light of our eternal nature, there is a dissolving of belief in separate identity. When you surrender, and in a sense are completely cleansed from the past, from memory, and this deep conditioning of the self, there is a new birth of being. At that time you see how there has never been a separate self in true reality. It was just a character in time, veiled in the illusion of a personal identification. There have been many changes of appearances, and many new expressions, all stemming from yourself, your eternal nature.

Life's sacred purpose is to realize your inner true nature of pure consciousness, evolving past the limitations of the body, the emotions, and the mechanism of thought. In truth your personality (body and mind), has its rightful place in the service of the true eternal self. Your true natural state is one of wholeness not separation, where there is not an ego state that dictates your life. In your true nature you are a pure witness to the transient nature of life, seeing clearly the illusion of temporary thoughts and emotions. Your natural expression is wisdom and clarity, where you are infinitely free.

As you become more deeply aware of your inner divinity, all expressions will become purified, reflecting your inner holiness. You will attain the ability to see the truth and remain steadfast in this inner-vision. In this vision from silence, thoughts become like fleeting butterflies, but never land in your consciousness. Despite all thoughts, your consciousness remains pure, untouched and free to be in its natural state of awareness. Letting go, of the identification with your personal self, is to merely relax into your true nature, effortlessly, allowing each precious moment to be filled with infinite possibilities. This divine practice, comes from surrender, not from effort, leading to a complete ease and peace of being. Living in your true essential nature, moment to moment, is to be firmly placed in act of divine witnessing, seeing through the illusion of life, uncovering the truth of being.

Meditation: On Emptiness

Breathing deeply, withdraw your senses from outward reality, turning inward, seeing all passing thoughts and emotions dissolve in the stillness of your sacred nature.

As you become more familiar with the vast, infinite space that resides within you will journey deeper and deeper to the source of your pure consciousness.

All comes from emptiness and all is returned to emptiness; the sacred source of life.

When the heart is breaking open, return to emptiness where you will receive peace, When the mind is restless and disturbed, return to emptiness where thought has no hold. When the soul yearns for deep nurturing return to emptiness where you drink from the chalice of life itself, the sacred source of emptiness.

Meditation is not a means

to an end,

It is both the means

and the end."

J. KRISHNAMURTI

CHAPTER FOURTEEN

THE INNER ASHRAM

Living in the Ashram Within
Contemplation of Truth
The Sacred Chalice of Life
Meditation: The Ashram Within

LIVING IN THE ASHRAM WITHIN

Deep within you, beneath the veil of the ego-self, is a being of profound wisdom and silence. You need not look outward to find it, it is always present in stillness. It is the essence of your heart, found when you retreat within and listen to the heart's holy song. As you take the journey to the ashram within, you can rest deeply, in oneness within your true nature. In your ashram within, the purity of your true nature will shine, as you let go of any residue of mistaken identity.

Daily life is one of outward expression, and an effort of survival for most people. Life has its innate suffering of old age, sickness, and death, teaching you to look to the meaning of this birth. Know deeply that by turning inward toward your divine nature, you will rest in your sanctuary of peace. A sanctuary, where you rest in the silence of your being, to receive the inner nourishing necessary to live life with strength and wisdom. When you walk in your ashram, you walk in the quietude of your true nature, allowing all expressions to come from that place.

The ashram within is our most treasured home in life, where you can find complete rest and renewal of being. Living in devotion to the ashram within we hold our precious energy there, no longer willing to believe in thoughts and emotions that are temporary in nature. There is an understanding that when caught in web of illusion, there is reaction, where your sacred energy is used in the misidentification process.

Your inner ashram awaits you, where you meet the teacher within the sacred heart of your being. It is here that silence is the key to the inner door, where your true home is waiting. Upon entry into your inner ashram, you will delight in the incredible beauty of your sanctuary, the melodious song of ancient wisdom, and the recognition that this is your true home. The ancient book of wisdom awaits you in the ashram within, where the story of your divine soul lives, and unfolds before your eyes. Your journey will take you to a place of no memory, no past, and no suffering, as the ashram within is the eternal emptiness of your being, where the personal self has merged with the divine.

The ashram within is a place of deep love and compassion, where you enter nakedly, leaving all facades of worldly identification behind. The ashram within is a place of supreme safety and security, as all things of this temporary world are no longer useful here, you can freely leave the burdens of the world behind. The holy ashram within is a place of absolute stillness, where the sound of the universe is heard, and the heartbeat of the infinite.

CONTEMPLATION OF TRUTH

In contemplation, you travel beyond the workings of the mind, into the silence and insight of being. In contemplation, all effort of becoming ceases; you merely recognize the source of your consciousness as divinity itself. Contemplation is the art of return to your true self, where you become deeply engaged in the nature of your true reality. The heart becomes still, thoughts become still, and the voice of the sacred is heard in the depth of your silence. All contemplation springs from silence where the wisdom of your inner master is heard. When the mind is silent, free from the voice of the personal self, a deep contemplation of the divine occurs.

The inquiry into your essential nature is a form of contemplating, thinking without any personal need to define yourself, or look for answers that will uphold your separate identity. Contemplation of truth is to dive deep into your heart for the answers of your being, turning away from the conditioning of the world. Living in meditation with your divine nature, allows you to experience the peace and holiness, of your being while living in the world. When you meet the inner guru of life within, you will see that all along you were walking hand in hand with this teacher, only the illusion of separation was in the way of this meeting.

Looking deep within your being, the center of your heart, you will find the truth of yourself that is the core of all human beings. This meeting allows you to perceive the profound oneness with all beings, knowing that the spark of the divine lives within all. In contemplation, you go beyond the limitation of conditioned thought into divine perception of truth.

The soul has journeyed into a physical form for the purpose of communing with the divine and to learn the test of separation. It is through contemplation that you tap the inner wisdom needed to understand this incarnation, and go beyond this temporary reality. Contemplation comes when you begin to investigate this temporary reality, having touched upon the source of truth. It is the supreme undertaking of your life to uncover the sacred that is always present. The love of your being will guide you to reveal this most precious life force, having no sentiment when it comes to letting go the false covering of the ego-self. This is the true love of the divine, when you turn away from what has obscured the vision of the truth. Through contemplation we journey beyond our physical thoughts, leaving all conditioning behind. We relax into the stillness of our being where our wisdom guide appears, life becomes a daily prayer and meditation with the divine.

Contemplation takes us to the point of stillness where understanding has reached its fullness, then the sacred guide becomes the voice of the silence within as you move into deeper and deeper perception.

THE SACRED CHALICE OF LIFE

Within you lives a sacred chalice, where you hold the wisdom of the divine. The chalice within holds the light of the world, the truth of your being. It is nurtured and kept in its fullness by silence, through devotion to your true nature.

The sacred chalice remains full when attention is no longer given to worldly identification, and you turn within where the chalice of life awaits. The sacred chalice is found in the silence and emptiness of the personal self that leaves all identification with the world behind.

When you realize that your true nature holds nothing, is nothing and contains nothing, there is a profound understanding that life is flowing through the emptiness of your being. The realization of the true self opens the awareness of presence, knowing that within our emptiness we commune with the divine. The sacred chalice of life is held in the temple within, always open for your return and renewal of spirit.

The sacred chalice within is always present, only dissipated by outward identification. When you feel that your being is in need of replenishing, return to the silence of your heart, where the sacred chalice of life renews your tired soul. The sacred chalice of life is where the holy waters pour the grace of wisdom and love into your being. The chalice within remains ever full, as you live in recognition of your sacred nature, walking in its purity. The chalice of life is the holy cup that contains the love of your being, infused by the love of the divine.

Meditation: The Ashram Within

The ashram within is your sanctuary of peace and silence, where the love of your true self, the wisdom of your divinity is available for your journey.

Know deeply that you can return at anytime to your living Ashram within, where you can drink from the sacred chalice of life.

Retreat within, to your inner ashram where you can renew, relax and commune with your divinity.

Return to the Ashram within as often as you wish, remembering what lives eternally is always found here.

All is Forgiveness...
A gift to yourself

COURSE IN MIRACLES W.103

CHAPTER FIFTEEN

DIVINE ENDEAVORS

Living in Goodness and Kindheartedness
The Source of Love Holds No Fear
Living with Unconditional Acceptance
Meditation: The Source of Love holds no Fear

LIVING IN GOODNESS AND KINDHEARTEDNESS

Deep inside, your true nature is a being of goodness and kindheartedness. What obscures this knowing is the conditioning of the personal self, who feels unworthy of the these divine gifts. The veils to the clear vision of your sacred self of goodness, are created from believing in yourself as a separate individual apart from the God-consciousness of your true nature. When you are exhausted from the personal journey that is bound by the illusion of time, memory, and striving, there is the natural turning within to your eternal nature. In this turning the veils of separation are removed as you meet your true self, the essence of goodness and kindness.

Goodness and kindness are expressions of your true nature, the gems of wisdom that make up the truth of your being. Until you are free from identification with the worldly self, there will be veils to these inner gems of your true nature. Look within, the heart for the self that is buried by thought and memory. Once there is looking, you can see, sense and feel the sacred being who lives deep within the heart. There is a intimacy of your true self of goodness and kindness, found in removing these veils created by misidentification.

The journey through visible reality, takes us through conditions that arise from the mass conditioning of our world, losing touch with our goodness. We learn at an early age to believe that we are body that needs to strive and survive, to deeply identify with its appearance, taking it to be the only reality. Emotions and thought play the part of the culprit in creating a web of identification that veils your true nature. This belief that we are separate, striving individuals takes us away from our true self, that is whole, and impersonal in nature. As we become more and more identified with the sense of a separate identity we lose contact with the eternal within, the heart of our being.

The sacred heart of our being is free from worldly identification and has the capacity of great love, kindheartedness, and goodness. Unfortunately, our true nature is veiled by the ignorance of the false self, and we are often unable to act out of the love of our hearts. Now, it is time to move away from the flock, and walk alone in your goodness and truth. For this action to occur, you must see clearly that you are responsible for your own relationship to inner truth and divinity. In knowing your true self within, you will automatically begin to honor and become devoted to your holiness and goodness.

In deep silence, the goodness of your being is cultivated, ready for life's purpose at any given moment. Goodness is found in the simplicity of your heart, when the heart is quiet, resting in its own wisdom. Goodness is found when there is surrender of the personal will to the greater will of your divinity. The life of the open heart to live a life of goodness, acting according to the love of the heart, which is beyond personal love and self-gratification. Love in this way never has its personal agenda, and is free to respond in the moment.

Goodness is congruent with kindheartedness, for they are the sprouts of divine love. In living from the love of your being, there is the birth of kindness in any moment that calls for it. Kindheartedness is to live in harmlessness, and touch people with your angelic wings as you pass them by in life.

Trust in Yourself, you are a being of goodness beyond your known comprehension, and you are capable of unconditional love and kindness, when you let go of all conditioning from the past. The gifts of the spirit await your return to what is always present, the light of your true nature. When you turn your attention away from your known reality, you will venture to your unknown reality. Going within, to the temple of silence you will uncover an array of beautiful gifts of your spirit. These gifts are packaged in divine love, with ribbons of your truth and wisdom, sealed with your true essence of goodness. When there is complete surrender to the truth of your being, your life becomes an expression of goodness and kindness.

The Source of Love Holds No Fear

What is fear other than the holding onto the mistaken identity, brought on by deep conditioning and thought? When there is fear, there is a separate individual person, who believes that there is something to lose, to protect, something to hold onto. The separate individual that is guided by time, memory and sorrow, is never really able to live in the present moment, because attention is going to the past and the projection of fear.

The separate individual judges what is appearing now, by the measure stick of the past, creating a web of thought that has its roots in fear. The thoughts that come from this deep identification, are fear of life's temporary changing nature, and a desire to hold onto outward security. See deeply, that you are not bound by fear, and that your true reality is found in the love of your being. Courage is found in abundance in the heart that knows its source of freedom is love, where there are no pulls toward outward identification. Courage is greatly needed for the brave being who turns away from the deep conditioning of humanity, letting go of all attachments that bind you to fear. Your inner guide is the essence of love and this love will guide you to see that fear is born from separation.

Upon turning within, to your sacred nature of love, all fear is dissolved in the light of your being. The fears that have been created through memory and time are cast aside as you see truly that the self that has held these fears for lifetimes, does not exist in truth. What is found within your eternal nature is untouched by fear, and all that comes from fear. There is the realization of your eternal consciousness, seeing that this sacred energy is unbound by anything and carries only the essence of pure love. In this pure love all fear is dissolved, and only silence remains.

When you know deeply that the only true meaning to life is to meet that which lives on in eternity, beyond the temporary conditions of this world, you begin to surrender your personal hold onto life. You begin to live in surrender to the holiness of life, seeing clearly the temporary nature of life. The nature of change is the only thing that you can really count on in this manifested world, so it is important to turn within, to the eternal nature of life, where you are at home, no matter what outer changes take place. Living in the light of your inner truth and essence of love is to live in complete surrender of the moment, dissolving all sense of separation into the oneness of sacred consciousness.

LIVING IN UNCONDITIONAL ACCEPTANCE

Living in unconditional acceptance you are surrendered to the eternal truth of life, recognizing your true nature of silence. You remain present to this changing reality, and the array of possibilities it manifests, trusting in the sacred force of the divine.

Living in unconditional acceptance of life is surrendering to each moment, with your divine witness in place, and whatever comes and goes, there is no personal suffering individual who experiences loss or gain. Unconditional acceptance is to embrace pain and sorrow with equal equanimity, knowing from the wisdom of your heart, that truth is found in the eternal source of life.

Unconditional acceptance is to live your life in the deep compassion of your spiritual heart, accepting all, the most painful of circumstances as well as the most pleasurable. In this acceptance you neither contract because of the pain nor project the desire of pleasure. Each moment is honored from the truth within, where you refer back to the unchanging nature of stillness.

Unconditional acceptance is to embrace your feelings of sadness, pain, desire or passion and completely allow the body to feel all, letting it go through you, without leaving an impression on your being. Unconditional acceptance is to fully embrace the results of all actions created from mistaken identification. It is to accept fully that you are truly a divine being, untouched by the past and forgiven by the divine witnessing of your true nature, this witnessing sets you free.

Meditation: The Source of Love Hold No Fear

Deep inside your being, there is a sacred thread to the eternal wisdom of the infinite.

Retreat within to your source of knowing, and you will meet your inner-most being, the essence of love itself.

Bring to the love of your divine being, all residues of fear that have been created by separation.

Allow any fear that comes to be immersed in the Love that lives within, for your true reality is that you are an embodiment of the divine.

In your truth you are whole, and your nature is the essence of love, where all fear is dissolved.

Know that at anytime you can bring all fear to the source of love within and delight in the submerging of it. For the Source of all love holds no fear.

I died as a mineral and became a plant,

I died as plant and rose to animal,

I died as animal and I was a man,

Why should I fear? When was I less by dying?

RUMI

CHAPTER SIXTEEN

THE CHRIST WITHIN

Letting the "I" Die on the Cross
Living in Reverence
The "Ever-Present" Eternal Presence
Meditation: Eternal Presence

LETTING THE "I" DIE ON THE CROSS

From a deep sense of mistaken identity, most of our life is spent in becoming something in the world. We truly believe that we are measured by our status, our accomplishments, our money, our bodies, our intellect and so on. It is by great grace that this outward pursuit of the self ceases, and you turn inward. Upon turning inward, you uncover the miracle of your eternal nature. The meeting of the your true nature within, happens of itself where there is a surrender of your false identification.

When you live in surrender to the Christ within, there is a sense of dying to the deep patterns and conditioning in your life. The inner death of what is false within feels as if there is a stripping away at your being, but it is merely a release of false identity. When you turn within, the familiar identity with your temporary nature begins to fall away, leaving you to face the emptiness of the self. This emptiness can be very frightful for the person who lives life for stimulation and gratification of self centered desires.

Most of life is spent in seeking, finding, running away and then seeking once more. This activity is highly charged with sensation and stimulation. When you begin to inquire into the nature of truth, there is an uncovering of a great force of stillness. The stillness of your true nature is revealed when the ego-self is silenced by the force of your sacred being, creating an inner death to what has been identified with through time and memory. This apparent death is the letting go of the manipulation of the ego-self in your life, freeing you to live in your true nature each precious moment. The dying on the cross is a metaphor for the death of your false holdings, attachments and conditioning that you have identified with so deeply as true reality.

Lifetimes have been spent where human beings have been in a constant state of seeking happiness and fulfillment from sense gratification. It is rare for a human to stop the trend of outer looking and turn within to perceive the meaning of this birth. All the seeking in the world becomes false when you discover that what has been sought all along is the eternal nature of the true self. The deep and profound process of healing misidentification, takes your life and cleanses it at the very core.

The dying to the old, and rebirth of the new is the organic process of the life force, that moves from the temporary to the eternal. When you recognize the true self within the temple of the heart there is a letting go, leading you to complete freedom of being. Surrendering to the unknown, opens your heart to your ever-present eternal nature. There is a deep sense of honor and devotion to the sacred that arises, feeling deeply grateful for the grace of recognition. You begin to live a daily life of prayer, in devotion to the unfolding process of your inner divinity.

As the recognition of your true Christ nature deepens, through the continual letting go, you will evolve into lighter and lighter aspects of your being. Allowing your separate individual identity to die on the inner cross of your Christ light, will assist this ascension to your ever-evolving sacred nature. There is no end or no beginning on this eternal journey, it is the luminous vehicle of the divine taking you into the infinite.

When you surrender all to the silence of being, the gems of wisdom are revealed, guiding you safely to your sacred resting place. There is a great cleansing from the holy waters found within, clearing all residues of misidentification away. The inner eye of wisdom opens, giving you the gift of great discernment, to see the false clearly, and the courage to turn toward the sacred truth of your being. Through the process of revealing your innermost self, you will touch upon the stream of holy consciousness, your Christ nature, connecting you to universal wisdom.

When you are born anew, your life is no longer your own, you are surrendered to the pure consciousness of the divine. When you let go of all personal holdings, there is only oneness with your divine source, this is the eternal freedom that has always been present.

LIVING IN REVERENCE

When awakened to your true nature, there is a new found freedom never experienced before, as all identification of the unreal falls away. There is a merging of your consciousness to divine emptiness of being, uncovering a deep humility from the knowledge that there is no longer a personal self in charge.

Identification with the temporary nature of life, is lifted as you realize that you are no longer the one who claims anything; successes are gone, failures are gone, enlightenment is gone, and ignorance is gone. All is gone in the emptiness of the personal self, and your divine nature reveals its unbounded, and ever-unfolding beauty.

In the recognition of your true nature, a great humility is awakened that impacts upon your daily functioning. There is no longer a person who lives in the effort of life, the will of silence now directs your being. The voice of silence is your inner guide, always accessible when you retreat into the stillness of your true nature. Listening to the voice of the silence will deepen your understanding of the sacred in life, leading you to live a life in reverence to the sacred that is behind the creation of life.

Living in reverence is to have the deepest respect that all is pure consciousness in our true reality.

The "ever-present" Eternal Presence

What lives within your being is the eternal presence, found in the temple of your spiritual heart, accessible through the silence of the self.

The worldly self is by nature emptiness, but what lives within is full, complete and flowing, when you are in communion with the source of your being, the eternal presence. The eternal nature of your being is a fragment of God, in which your consciousness is the consciousness of the infinite. Each small self is born from separation, resulting in a protective ego that strives to remain alive, holding this reality as real. Each fragment of separation is dissolved in sacred consciousness, as the greater becomes the whole, the wave becomes the sea.

The eternal presence within is your resting place of comfort and silence, where there is strength to overcome even the greatest sorrow. In silence you are able to face all difficulties in the light of the eternal presence, seeing all of creation as the unfolding grace of God, leading to deeper and deeper wisdom. All difficulties in life have their roots in lifetimes of identification with the separate ego-self. In the light of the eternal presence, you walk with your eternal companion, knowing that the cyclic nature of life, continues through the process of outward change, bound by time. The sacred presence that is alive in the silence of being, is always there to comfort and to renew your eternal being. Whatever is needed for the healing of misidentification is found within, as you turn to the ever-present, sacred source of your being.

Meditation: Eternal Presence

 As you turn inward to your eternal presence, away from appearances, the illusion of time, you will journey deep into the silence of your luminous heart.

Surrender your being to the eternal presence of your spiritual heart. Know this presence as your eternal companion.

This sacred presence is always with you, holding you, guiding you and protecting you.

The presence within, is found when you journey into the stillness of your being.

It is here you will find a light glowing held by the hand of the beloved who waits for your return. Know that you are always held in this most holy hand.

Know the mirror of the heart is infinite,

Either the understanding falls silent,

or it leads you astray, because the heart is with God,

or indeed the heart is He.

RUMI

CHAPTER SEVENTEEN

ONENESS OF BEING

Living in Wholeness
Healing the Separate Sense of Self
The Light of the Soul
Meditation: The Celestial Light of Oneness

LIVING IN WHOLENESS

Living in wholeness is to recognize the wholeness within, with a conscious awareness of the fragmented nature of life. When the separate individual recognizes that their true nature is wholeness, there is a release of all things held in separation. Healing is from the love of the true being who lives within. All becomes whole; all that is born of separation ends.

Where there is wholeness, there is no separation, no judgment and complete compassion for all living things, seeing all as one. Where there is wholeness, there is a sense of being one with all of life, where the errors of the personal self are not identified as real. The recognition of the true self within, brings you back to wholeness, and you live your life as a whole human being. You see that the true nature of all beings is pure and holy consciousness, and in that seeing all separation is dissolved.

Living in wholeness is viewing life as complete and whole just that way it is and not pursuing anything from a view point of lack. Living in wholeness is to live your life in direct relationship with your spiritual heart and the truth of your being. This requires a deep sincerity to live according to the dictates of the heart and listen very carefully within to the will of the silence.

Listening within to the will of silence, creates a wholeness of being for you no longer listen to the fragmented ego-self, with its deep habit of following thought and emotion outward. Your wholeness is always been present, but the illusion of the separate self has created a block to its clear vision. When you realize that there is only pure consciousness of which we are created from, we return to the beauty of the whole, the sacred source of all beings.

Living in wholeness is to live in your purity and live in the perfection of your being which is a natural expression of your sacred consciousness. Your wholeness is always present, without effort its beauty unfolds before your eyes. When the personality retreats to the stillness within there is complete recognition of your true home, all fragments become one with the whole of consciousness. When you realize that the true self within is pure consciousness, the wisdom of your higher intelligence is activated and the personal will is transformed to Divine Will. You experience a transformation of the self as the identification with a personal identity, evolves to more beauty, and greater understanding and compassion of being. The realized self is whole and complete unto itself, and one with the source of consciousness.

HEALING THE SEPARATE SENSE OF SELF

Your inner being has been neglected for far too long, while giving attention to the ego-self that in reality is a product of thought, projection and memory. What lives within you is whole, complete and a spark of the divine, rarely met by most in a lifetime. The person who believes in a separate identity, often lives a life in the pursuit of power and self attainment. This is the root of all karmic activity, where the personal self lives enduring the cycles of pleasure and pain, gain and loss, and is bound through desire to these cycles. Bondage is through belief in this separate way of being, based on time and memory, and the constant pursuit of self-gratification. When the belief in this separate individual as the controller in your life ends, you turn to stillness within where a deep and profound healing takes place.

The quest for the loss sense of self begins at the age where most people begin to think and feel for themselves, searching for identity and meaning from this temporary world. The search brings you to temporary happiness, temporary gratification of desire, authority, and the never ending pursuit to fill an empty well. The empty well is in fact truly empty and never can be filled by this outward search, the miracle is found by turning within where the sacred source of your being replenishes your self.

Most of life is spent ignoring the call of the soul within, until the light of yearning is dimmed. There is a complete compromise of your life, the veils to your true nature become multi-layered as you live your life in a deep forgetting of what is real. The forgetting of your true nature creates a sense of unworthiness, as the fragmented self seeks to validate its reality throughout life. You live your life in compliance with the false, creating a deeper sense of untruth and self betrayal. This self that seeks gratification to fulfill itself, has created a vast river of separation from the true self that remains, in the silence of your heart. Healing the fragmented being will wash away all residue of the past, allowing you to live in the current moment in complete freedom from conditioning. This healing is readily found by turning toward the wholeness and holiness of your true ever-abiding nature, leaving the past behind.

Life when lived from wholeness, is a life that is alive, vitally energized for each moment. In turning your attention inward, the very act of looking brings the light of healing to all that is held in separation. This eternal light of your true nature, heals all fragmentation, unifying you with the source of pure consciousness.

THE LIGHT OF THE SOUL

Through lifetimes of mistaken identity, our true essence is veiled by the ignorance of the personal ego-self. When we cease to identify with the ego-self, we open the channel for the light of the soul to come through, and the unfolding to the core of your being takes place. In life, there is a great deal of sorrow, unhappiness and suffering, that is born from mistaken identity and false conditioning.

Viewing life from the true inner self, is to see how sorrow plays an important part in the lessons of the individual. When we are enmeshed in our ego-self, we live a life according to pleasure and pain. Sorrow from this level is never-ending, for you can never be free from cause and effect, as long as you are rooted in identification with the separate individual. Sorrow of a personal nature subsides when you discover that the true self is found by a simple turning away from the outer to the inner.

When we live life in identification with our body and mind, we experience limitation, constriction, and a lack of understanding of our true nature. We live our life in service to the physical, emotional and mental expressions, and our true nature that is whole, undivided within, is buried in false identification. When the meeting with our true nature occurs, identification with the outer reality, is seen through the light of your soul. Upon meeting your true essence within, a deep longing to remain in your pure nature becomes a daily prayer. The familiar pulls continue to bring you back into the limitation of a separate individual, such as fear, attachment, and worry. Remember your true nature, and seek within to have the vigilance required to slay the illusion of the ego-self with all its expressions rooted in fear. Keep the light burning, by believing in nothing other than your own inner light, nurturing it, keeping it bright through devotion to its truth.

Harmlessness becomes an important act of consciousness, as you see the importance of true caring in the world of thoughts, words and deeds. When awakened to your true nature, life becomes a quest to live in service to this suffering world, going beyond self needs, helping others along the way. A great compassion develops deep within the heart, leading you to understand the imperfections of this temporary manifestation. When there is an awareness of what is real and everlasting; your true nature, you can live in the world in a tentative way, in constant reference to the wisdom of silence.

We conquer the nature of fear, by seeing clearly that fear comes from believing in the illusion that we are our thoughts, our emotions or our physical body. Fear is based on separation, when there is a realization that there is no separation, fear is immersed in the love of your true sacred nature. Life brings us to the deep feeling of gratitude, seeing all as God's will, being grateful for what is true, eternal and sacred.

The mastery process requires an inner strength that is generated by your truth. We learn the art of looking inward, gradually increasing steadfastness in looking, in observation, until there is no looking or observing, there is just being. This is when you drop all effort to observe, where the observer and the observed become a unified whole. When the light of the soul is at its brightest there is no more thought about the self in any way, the self is neither free or bound, neither separate or whole. Your true being is an open channel to the light of the divine, where all is transformed in silence.

Meditation: The Celestial Light of Oneness

 Breathe deeply and relax into the heart of your true knowing. Turn within, letting go all effort, you begin to feel a deep relaxation as you disengage from outer reality.

The light within, reveals and shines as you expand into the relaxation and inner peace of your infinite being.

The light within, has greater and greater luminosity, as you deepen your silence, surrendering all to this light .

This luminosity is the celestial light of oneness, the light of the world and all beings.

Your shining light touches the world, when the radiance of your being is uncovered shining brightly on your sacred path.

The Celestial Light of oneness, unifies us all. This is the guiding light of the world.

You are the notes, and we are the flute,

We are the mountain, you are the sounds coming down.

We are the pawns and kings and rooks

We are lions rolling and unrolling on flags

Your invisible wind carries us through the world.

RUMI

Chapter Eighteen

GIFTS OF THE SPIRIT

Sacred Living, Beauty, Our Celestial Song
Deep Gratitude and Humility, Communion with the Divine
Happiness and Joy, Delighting in Spirit
Meditation: The Gifts of the Spirit

Sacred Living, Beauty, Our Celestial Song

Sacred Living, is to live life from wholeness, beauty and in deep gratitude for all things. Sacredness in daily life is living each moment in reverence, seeing the incredible holiness in life. When you touch into the sacred, a deep communion with life begins, creating a sense of unity and oneness in daily life, and the appreciation for beauty.

Beauty is living in grace, fully appreciating all of manifestation, seeing goodness in this manifested world. Beauty within is like being bathed in the brilliance of God's creation, expanding into the infinite consciousness of being. Opening like a flower, unfolding to your inner beauty, is living this sacred life fully.

You are beauty itself when your identification and attention shifts from what is subject to time, to the timelessness of your inner true nature, where you are infinitely free. All of the beauty of life is found within, as you live from your wholeness, you are one with the magnificent oceans, the splendid array of nature, the grandness of this earth's unfathomable beauty.

The celestial song of the divine creates melodies unheard by most ears, melodies that portray the beauty and grace of life. The song of life teaches us to just observe, to trust that we are in the hands of something larger, more magnificent than our small selves could ever fathom. Listen to the celestial song of the divine, found in the stillness of the heart. A song that will inspire you to live life according to your innermost truth, a song that teaches about the joy of the divine, and the beauty of surrender. Living in beauty is to know beauty as your true nature, honoring it in your daily life.

You are the bouquet of flowers given to the holy spirit within, you are the beauty of the sea, where the wave knows its source is the ocean itself, you are the grandeur of the mountain, knowing that the first step up the mountain is the same as the arrival. You are the love in a child's heart, knowing that wonder and innocence is your true nature. You are the beauty of your daily life, where each moment is precious, when lived to the tune of your Celestial Song.

DEEP GRATITUDE AND HUMILITY, COMMUNION WITH THE DIVINE

Gratitude is a natural blossoming of the understanding of your true nature. Life becomes a daily blessing, pointing to the true source of your being. Painful experiences, joyful experiences, all become apart of the great play of divinity; each of life's experiences contain the miracle of truth. Grace is the force that reveals the truth in your personal suffering, the force that strips the self down to the core of its divine nature.

Gratitude is being deeply thankful for the daily opportunity, to see the sacred consciousness of life, in all beings and in yourself. Living in gratitude is to experience the sacred in life, honoring and expressing it throughout all changes. Gratitude is seeing that we have been blessed with a span of time to realize the reason for this birth. To look within and discover the sacredness of being, seeing all as sacred, and to walk in deep reverence of the divine force behind all of manifestation.

Living in gratitude of life's holy teaching is to give up the self-centered way of being and turn within, in great humility. We are blessed beyond comprehension to know this birth as a revelation of the divine seeing all as this revelation. In gratitude of the heart we see how suffering and sorrow play a part in revealing the divine in life. All of suffering contains a message within, guiding you to your true nature of strength and eternal wisdom. Living in gratitude is to see no matter how painful life is, you are able to look and see the divine blessing that is being revealed. Gratitude is to accept blessings in whatever form they appear in, seeing life's guidance as a message of the divine.

Gratitude deepens in your heart, as you appreciate all of life's blessings, seeing all as an unfolding miracle. Knowing deep gratitude within, is honoring each precious moment, seeing each moment as a wonderful opportunity to be one with truth. Gratitude is an acknowledgment of grace in your daily life, seeing the outer manifestation as an opportunity to live in the grace of being.

Life is a miracle, gratitude deepens as we see the miraculous nature of life and recognizing the divine energy behind manifestation. The foundation for gratitude is deep humility, living in reverence of life, trusting the sacred movement behind life. Humility is when there is a vigilant awareness of the separate sense of self, with a constant return to emptiness, the nature of our reality. Life becomes a deepening of gratitude knowing that when you turn to the emptiness of the self within, the miracle of the divine appears.

Looking at the vastness of this creation, how can we not be humble to this great force that is behind all of creation? When we acknowledge that we are nothing in the eyes of the world, we let go of the self the way we have known it to be, and experience our true essence, which is just spacious awareness. Letting go, allows you to relax into your sacred force, and experience a deep communion with the eternal.

HAPPINESS AND JOY, DELIGHTING IN SPIRIT

The journey of a being in this physical body often creates a pattern for outward searching to find meaning and happiness. You can spend a whole lifetime seeking happiness in many different ways, never finding fulfillment in this pursuit. When the seeking turns to exhaustion from worldly effort and striving, you have the opportunity to turn within, to the grace of being. Turning within, to your true nature which is always present will lead you all the happiness that is inherent in your being.

Happiness is found in simply being, a place where emotions and thoughts are stilled, and efforts of the personal self are calmed. You are the very essence of happiness and joy, for what is behind all of your thoughts, emotions and physical sensations is the flow of life itself, your sacred true nature.

In your truest being, you are a song of joy to the divine, rejoicing in the simplest display of life, the beauty that is before you. There are no conditions that you must have in order to be happy, in fact all conditions must be dropped, you just need to turn inward and merge with the happiness of your true nature. Happiness is found in the song of your heart, when the burden of worldly identification is left behind.

Happiness is your true nature, untouched by thought, emotions and the conditioning from the past. You are a whole human being, whose happiness is found by turning within and recognizing your true nature of divinity. Upon this recognition, live in devotion to the source of your divinity. This is where all true joy and happiness are found; this is the gift of this birth.

Meditation: The Gifts of Spirit

 Look within and see the beautiful being who resides in the temple of your spiritual heart.

Know that your true nature is a being of love, wisdom, compassion and peace; the gifts of the spirit.

When life sends a lesson of humility, turn within and listen to your inner voice. See that Humility is the grace that strips away any veils to your true nature.

When life sends you a lesson in Gratitude, turn within and listen to your inner voice.

Gratitude is the grace that takes away any sense of being unmindful in your life.

Look within and meet the joyous being who sings a celestial song of beauty.

Spiritual growth may be measured

by a decrease of afflictive emotions and increase

of love and compassion for others.

CHAGDUD TULKU

CHAPTER NINETEEN

THE SONG OF THE HEART

Living in Devotion, Love of the Divine
Forgiveness and Compassion, Freeing the Heart from the Past
The Flowering of the Lotus Heart
Meditation: The Lotus of the Heart

LIVING IN DEVOTION, LOVE OF THE DIVINE

Great is the love force within all souls, a love that is deep and unlimited, found in the oneness of your sacred being. Love is the essence of pure consciousness, deepening as you unfold into the light of pure being. To love yourself is to love the eternal sacred force that is your true self, from this love comes the love of the divine. To love yourself is to recognize, the living divinity within, seeing that there is only oneness in truth. This love of your true self kindles a great devotion to the beloved within all beings, knowing that we all come from one source.

When there is a turning away from outer reality, the body, senses and emotions of the separate self, you turn inward to the source of love, wisdom and divinity. This turning away from worldly identification stems from a deep realization that true happiness is found in the kingdom within, resulting in a deep yearning for the divine. Suffering of a personal nature is no longer a reality as you become a devotee of the divine; your separate identity drowns in divine love. Life becomes a living prayer and communion with that which is sacred. Devotion is deepened in the recognition of the divine within, where all is held in silence. Living in devotion is to listen to the wisdom of the divine, in all walks of life. Devotion to the sacred source of life, is to return to the joy of pure being. This reservoir of joy sustains all.

A yearning for the beloved, a devotion to God, is all that is required to let go and let the river of grace carry you home. Leave behind all worldly identification with a separate self, surrendering to the sacred presence that lives within your heart. Know that as you realize your true self, you will walk in this world without the entanglement of worldly illusion, in this realization you are free.

Living in devotion is to see all as one being, to have a great compassion for yourself and for all beings, with an ever-deepening awareness of the suffering of this world. When you touch upon your own divinity there is a clear realization of the root cause of suffering; separation, and identification with that which is temporary. Turning within, you meet your eternal nature, you find complete rest, knowing this is the true home of all beings.

FORGIVENESS AND COMPASSION, FREEING THE HEART FROM THE PAST

Forgiveness of yourself and others is having the compassion to understand mistakes made from the illusionary self, and see in truth there is never any harm meant. All comes from ignorance when you walk in the mistaken identity of the self, all is forgiven when you turn to the light of your true nature.

Our human nature is deeply conditioned to live life in pursuit of self- gain and self- gratification, asleep to the true reality of pure consciousness. When you see the violence, brutality and deep cause of suffering that our ego-mechanistic behavior causes, a natural inquiry develops. Asking yourself who you are in truth, is the most essential question to finding out the cause of suffering in your personal life and in the world. Going within, you access the love and wisdom of your heart, where all is forgiven, as you live in the light of your true nature .

In contemplation, you can clearly see how individual selves, in the pursuit of self-gain have caused untold harm to themselves and to fellow beings. This conditioning of humanity has its roots in the past, carrying the legacy of suffering to all beings on life's journey. The love of truth and awareness of the divine nature of life, will assist each being to end this sorrowful process of false identification.

The nature of the mistaken identity is often hurtful, stemming from the deep conditioning of its separateness, and needing to hold onto some position. When this identification ends, the illusion of the past with all its memories end, leading you to understand the profound meaning of life in the current moment. Forgiveness allows you to start over both in yourself, and in relationship to others.

Observe how your liberation from the past quickly comes into play when you practice the art of forgiveness. Practicing forgiveness in your life requires you to not only have deep compassion for yourself, but also for the relationships you have had throughout your life. Deep compassion opens the heart to the understanding that all beings are essentially divine and mistakes are born from the ignorance of this divinity. Compassion leads you to a greater understanding of the inner divinity within all beings, while observing the nature of the imperfect self that is caught in illusion.

Forgiveness leads you to the light of the true self that is ever-abiding in each sacred moment. This moment, which has its foundation in eternity, can only bring a rebirth of the new, free from all past conditions.

Your true nature is gifted with the wisdom of the divine and a heart of great understanding and compassion, unconditionally accepting whatever comes or goes in life. You are able to see clearly where the error in identification lies and where the mistaken beliefs are. You are then able to see the display of emotional states that come and go as well as the changing nature of life, while remaining in your true self of witness consciousness.

Having compassion is to understand the spiritual heart of your true being and that of others, knowing that the suffering that all humans partake of is one of not knowing the true nature of the self. All sorrow stems from this ignorance. You can only have compassion for what is not seen, not recognized. Compassion is to see the conditioning of the false self, understanding the only way out of suffering is to realize the self in its true reality.

Observe passing thoughts and feelings such as fear, doubt, hatred, and jealously, and see when you participate in these temporary states how it creates a traumatic energy in the moment. With the compassionate heart you can observe when your personality consciousness is entertaining passing emotions and thoughts, while witnessing from your true nature. This observation will assist you in disengaging in the belief of these passing states, knowing deeply, the infinite source of your being. In this way you will allow these temporary states to pass and your true self will remain strong, untouched, the true master of any situation.

Each moment is an opportunity to observe from your true self, and act accordingly to the dictates of your true self. When that does not happen lovingly and with compassion, look within and heal the separation that is created from the split of the personality consciousness and the divine consciousness. In the compassionate heart you are able to see what is to be learned from the situation. Learning comes from detachment of the self, a willingness to honor the truth of life. Each moment is the opportunity to return to the wholeness and truth of your sacred being, expressing your thoughts and emotions from this pure state.

In the compassionate heart you find humility, knowing that you always have the opportunity to learn, and to start "anew" in any given situation. Forgiveness of yourself and others is a powerful tool, bringing all of yourself to the current moment. Allow the flow of life's grace to deepen your understanding of your self, therefore deepening the understanding of all beings. This sacred flow of life raises your self, to the light of your pure consciousness, healing all past impressions.

True service is uncovering your divine nature now, sharing your essential being with the world. Your being is one with the divine consciousness of life, guided to fulfill your sacred destiny, in this way it is essential for you to truly know and trust yourself.

Compassion sees all with deep understanding eyes, and knows that underneath the appearance of things, we are all one. Compassion is the expression of deep unconditional love, a love that sees only the eternal divine reality, recognizing that all beings are this truth. Compassion is the utmost respect for divine energy, seeing the eternal nature of all beings, seeing the oneness of life. Allow your heart to open to its true flowering, of wisdom, light and compassion, seeing this suffering world is a result of the compassion heart being closed to this flowering.

Compassion leads you to deeper oneness with your true essence, and to the essence of all living beings. Let go and surrender all areas in your life that are not in harmony with your pure consciousness. In the compassionate heart there is an awareness that all errors are born from the mistaken identity that we take ourselves to be. The truth of all beings is that we are pure divine consciousness and the light of Christ resides within our spiritual heart, this light expresses goodness, beauty and the eternal wisdom and love.

THE FLOWERING LOTUS OF THE HEART

The lotus of the heart, is forever flowering unto its natural beauty. Within the core of your heart is a sacred resting place where you can retreat to in silence; finding the pure love, pure wisdom, and guidance of your true self. As each petal unfolds within the heart, the sacred chalice of life is filled.

The flowering lotus of the heart brings you into wholeness and divine wisdom, as each petal gently unfolds; you travel deeper into the silence of the heart. As the petals of the flowering heart open, there are greater levels of awareness of your true nature. The flowering of the heart opens in rhythm to the natural evolution of being. It is only when an individual turns away from their true self, that the flowering of the heart temporarily ceases its natural unfolding process. When your attention is turned from outward identification to the sacred being within, the inner truth becomes the nurturing for the flowering of the heart. The flowering lotus of the heart is the letting go of all misidentification, deepening the recognition of your true nature.

The lotus of the heart is unfolding to your higher nature; the stem is rooted in the divine, while the petals represent your inner flowering.

The first unfolding petal is when you meet your innermost self within the sanctuary of your heart, awareness turns from identification with the body, to knowing your true self.

The second unfolding petal opens through the realization that you are not your emotions. As you express the qualities of beauty, joy and love in your life, emotions are an expression of your true nature, not of the ego-self.

The third petal unfolds in the lotus of the heart when thinking is used for higher aspiration, and the mind becomes an instrument to reach clearer understanding of divinity. The mind becomes a silent observer, thinking stems from intuition, perception and discernment.

The fourth petal opens when you release attachment to the things of this world. The knowledge obtained within the hearts unfolding lotus deepens your understanding of pure consciousness.

The fifth petal unfolds when you are firmly embedded in your true nature, demonstrating steadfastness, vigilance, and uncompromising clarity of your true nature. Your emotional nature finds its expression in love, bring a wellspring of beauty to your life.

The sixth petal unfolds when all that is not of your pure consciousness is burned in the sacred fire of your inner light.

The seventh petal opens when your inner nature becomes all inclusive, infused with divine love, harmlessness, and adoration for the divine.

The eight petal opens when there is a direct perception of your true reality.

The ninth petal opens when there is deep and profound peace, and the past is dissolved completely.

Meditation: The Lotus of the Heart

The beauty of your being is ever-unfolding, in the lotus of your heart.

Go within, to the flowering of your soul, and see each petal of your being as unfolding in the beauty of your true nature.

Each petal is your inner gift to yourself and to the eternal presence of life.

You are a sacred lotus, whose stem is rooted in the earth with your ever-unfolding petals reaching to the infinite.

God's grace is the beginning, the middle, and the end.

When you pray for God's grace, you are like someone standing

neck-deep in water and yet crying out for water.

It is like saying that someone neck-deep in water

feels thirsty, or that a fish in water feels thirsty,

or that the water feels thirsty.

RAMANA MAHARSHI

CHAPTER TWENTY

GRACE

The Sacred River of Grace
Accept the Calling
The Timeless Flow of Life
Meditation: Stillness

THE SACRED RIVER OF GRACE

Grace is the sacred river behind all of life. It flows in its mysterious way through your lifetime, guiding you, assisting you in the revelation of true reality. All of life's difficulties are disguised in grace, each painful experience leads you closer to your eternal stillness of truth and wisdom, healing the cause of sorrow.

Pain and suffering are the result of great grace, showing you where your life needs more love, more attention. Grace is seeing yourself with total honesty, having the humility to take what is seen, knowing that the veil of ignorance that covers your true essence does not exist in reality. Grace is seeing that life is a continuous pointer to your true reality, timeless and eternal, and that all errors are born from separation from your true reality.

Humility and grace are cultivated from knowing that your true essence is divine and eternal, seeing that expressions from your personality nature, are not always in the light of your divine nature. Grace is the clear observation of that which is false, seeing that truth is found in turning away from a separate identity. It is a deep letting go of all that is not of your true self, opening to the light of your pure consciousness.

Grace is allowing all the accumulated memories from the past to dissolve in the sacredness of your true self. Grace is your inner guide that leads you to look beyond the personal and see your true essential nature. Grace, comes in the form of gentle reminders, and grace is the fearless force of cutting of the false.

Whether grace shows itself in the form of the gentleness of a divine mother, or the fierceness of the divine father, all should be welcomed, in assisting you in uncovering the veils to your real self. Grace may come at moments when least expected, when you are blessed with unseen guidance to assist you in remaining true to yourself.

See all as grace, even the most humbling of situations and the darkest and empty moments, for life always has its divine hand in the one who has taken the fork off the path of the personal self. All that occurs in life is by the sacred force of Grace.

Grace is the divine force underneath all of life's circumstance, whether it is pleasant or unpleasant, go beyond what is personally satisfying, see the unchanging nature of life as divine grace.

The sacred river of grace flows in all beings lives, and is accessible by simply turning within, and letting go of personal striving. Grace is the blessing of life itself, our very breath, the beat or our hearts, all is given from the generous nature of grace.

All are miracles in the light of grace, the smile of a child, the love of an elder, the touch of a friend, the truth that is shared amongst souls of God. Grace is the miracle of life. When there is a letting go of your personal identification, exposing all in the sacred river, the swift current of grace takes you home. This mysterious force is the grace behind everything. Grace is always moving in our lives, guiding, protecting and providing for us.

Grace has a direct relationship with faith, allowing that which is unseen and sacred to take care of our souls. Trusting in that which is eternal, and surrendering to the quiet voice within, leading you to the sacred resting place of your inner being, where complete peace abides.

Grace is the sacred force that guides us home to our inner truth, the core of our being. Life continues on, time moves on, experiences come and go, but the true essence within is eternal, beyond all conditions of time. Grace is the everlasting awareness of your true nature, living in the peace and love of its blessing.

Your natural state is wholeness, one with the source of life. As a spark of this oneness, your expression from your individual identity is merely a reflection of your eternal being, deep within your heart. Grace is the force that calls all souls home to rest in their own divinity. Listen to the voice of grace, see what part of you is yearning for the beloved within, your ever abiding Christ light. The very yearning for that which is real, sacred and eternal, is the work of grace. When your mistaken identity no longer dictates your daily life, grace reveals your true nature, free from all states, all experiences, and conditions in time. Lifetimes have been spent in the familiar territory of the body, mind, and senses, which can be viewed as the rocks, the forks, the individual objects of the river. Now it is time to see the essence of the sacred river life in its wholeness. In seeing this essence, you are propelled to dive into its current, which is beyond the personal will of separation. The river of grace is the current of life, the very current of your being, and will dissolve all seeds of sorrow in its mightiness.

The sacred river of grace asks only that you trust the current that is the sacred source of life's creations. This trust is to surrender your life to this sacred source, letting all go into the river of grace.

ACCEPT THE CALLING

Lifetimes have been lived in devotion to the belief in our separate existence, attaining power from the image of our self. Very few beings have stopped the projection of the self long enough to reveal what lives within when all comes to silence, where the false sense of self is laid to rest. Our deep belief is that we are the sum total of our temporary state, such as the past, emotions, conditioning, memory, creating an identity that is based on thought.

Our misidentification creates a deep soul weariness, propelling our tired souls to search for truth and meaning in life. Through outward identification you are on the endless path of giving the sacred energy of life to the beliefs of your personal identification, leading you to a great exhaustion of your vital force. The revelation is: All searching ends when you turn within, and meet the true self that has been present all along. When there is a transformation of yourself, through the recognition that you are in reality an eternal being, not of this temporary world, you hear the sacred calling of your life. Accepting the calling is to listen to the voice of the silence within, surrendering to the divine guidance of truth and wisdom.

Accepting the calling is to stop the projections of the ego-self and return to the silence of being, where the holy presence awaits. Accepting the calling is to let go of all personal holdings to the river of grace, trusting in the divine current. In this most sacred river, you are cleansed from all separation, allowing the refreshing waters to renew all of your being.

THE TIMELESS FLOW OF LIFE

The illusion of life is that we are bound by any condition, is based on the thought of who we think we are. All human beings are graced with a great wisdom and ability to contemplate the real meaning of life, seeing that in truth we are a free being, flowing down the timeless river of life. When you have the intention for freedom, to discover the root cause of sorrow, there is a great vigilance in uncovering the truth.

You realize that happiness cannot be found when you are caught in conditions bound by time, memory and conditioning; real happiness is found by turning within to your timeless nature. Happiness is found when there is a complete letting go to the timeless of flow of life, where you see the light of the true self, is completely free from all conditions.

When you surrender to the timeless flow of life, energies are used in behalf of the eternal presence, and life is lived in devotion to everlasting divinity. When you learn that your true nature is the essence of the eternal, untouched by anything, you are no longer interested in the temporary gain of the world. A life lived in the world with a strong sense of self-realization is knowing at any time you can retreat into the silence of your being, where you unite with the timeless flow of life. Know deeply the truth of your being, use this life as the most precious opportunity to surrender any sense of separation to the timeless flow of life, realizing in unity you are a whole human being. Trust in Yourself !

Meditation: Stillness

There is an aspect of our consciousness that is quiet, unruffled by outward manifestation

Within Stillness of mind and emotions, the truth of your being is revealed.

Deep inside there is a movement of understanding, truth, timeless knowledge, that is accessed by this stillness

Consciousness change is within, stillness creating an unruffled pool for the souls reflection

It is within this quiet pool the true self reflects the light of divinity, transcending all the limitations of the world

In this transcendence we journey into stillness, the healing light of the soul

JAYA SARADA

INDEX

Oh Lord, dweller within
You are the light
In the hearts lotus,
Om is your very self,
Om, holiest word,
Seed and source of the scriptures,
Logic can never discover
You, Lord, but the yogis
Know you in meditation
In you are all God's faces,
His forms and aspects,
In you also
We find the guru,
In every heart you are
And if but once, only,
A man will open
His mind to receive you
Truly that man
is free forever

SHANKARA

A Note From The Editor

I started working on the editing process of **Trust in Yourself** during a death in my family. The few hours each day that I spent working on the manuscript was a time of mindful meditation. I traveled from my outward circumstance, toward the silence of my heart, guided by Jaya's words.

I saw Jaya's words live, as I was the divine witness to my sister's pain and profound grief.

I feel a deep sense of gratitude to Jaya, for her respect and humility toward her own work, as well as my own. I pass these prayers of wisdom back around to her, and our circle is complete. She has never wavered in her vision, yet she has remained truly open, allowing for the birth of her extraordinary work to take shape. I hope Jaya's words will be translated to all of you who read these words, from deep within the cave of your hearts. It is in that spacious and silent retreat, we will learn to trust again.

What is Grace?

Grace is in the wind,
Silent, stealthy, shrieking,
Yes, sometimes she shrieks,
Screaming air fills the sky,
Swirling up the storms of forgetting,
Moving the clouds quickly,
Across the face,
Of the moon, revealing a luminous gaze,
But only for a moment,
For the wind,
She is on the move,
Rocketing us all forward,
And backward, cleansed by her breath
Listening to her whispered longings,
We need her to move us along,
The divine breath that brings the air
From the temple, full of prayer,
Chants carried over oceans and vast continents,
To rest briefly on my porch, my portal,
Take a breath, it is all there,
Everywhere the wind has been.
The divine air rises and falls
Inside my chest cavity, cave of wonder,
Illuminating the four chambers,
With its own coursing wind.

JONI TAKANIKOS,
Editor of **TRUST IN YOURSELF**

ACKNOWLEDGEMENTS

The pathway of the soul is paved with blessings. It is a moving foundation illuminated by the grace that is ever-present, behind all of life's manifestation. Along this road we take to become a human being, live many guides who live in service; they point to the divine silence of our true abiding nature. I give deep appreciation and eternal gratitude for the following lights on the planet:

The Theosophical Society has nurtured me since early childhood:

Sri Ramakrishna and The Vedanta Society; The Teachings of the Buddha; The Teachings of Christ; A Course in Miracles; J. Krishnamurti; Sathya Sai Baba; The divine mother, Amachi; Ramana Maharshi; Papaji (HLW Poonja) Sri Nisaargadatta, and Sri Sankaracharya.

Deep gratitude to Hanuman and Gangiji, who in their deepest devotion they share the teachings of beloved Papaji and Ramana Maharshi.

All have pointed in the direction of self-realization and the meeting of the truth within. The doorway into the silence of being is open to all who knock, this is where all love springs forth, this love is the very foundation for this book.

My dearest Mother knew this love and lived it throughout her life. The life she has lived has been an example of living love and living truth. She found her divinity within at an early age and from this wisdom she reflected the truth in all beings that crossed her path. The search is not outside yourself; she boldly stated this truth to all her fellow travelers. You are already that which you search for. This was the seed I grew from and my search for the divine began and ended right in my own heart. Throughout my life I made several trips to India to seek a living master; I searched the earth for true meaning and sought the reason for living.

The search lead me to many spiritual studies, but it was only when I deeply understood that our true nature is one of God-consciousness and any outside attempt to find it will only be just another activity of the mind. I learned that the essence of truth is found by a simple turning within and relaxation into the silence of the heart. The truth is, our reality is unfathomable and is only found through inner exploration. We may spend years trying to get it, but the simplest more extraordinary fact is that it is within our being all along. It is the very breath we breathe, the very beat of our hearts, it is found in the silence of our being. When we listen to our inner divinity within us; the kingdom and all its treasures of truth are open to each human being. It is through this song of silence we come to touch divine grace. This work has been received from the silence of being, offered with great love. Throughout all of life's outward changes there is the eternal flame that burns in each heart. The luminosity of this flame is our guide-post to our sacred resting place within, it is here we are home.

about Grace Foundation

The vision of Grace Foundation is to be a guidepost for all beings on the journey of life. We believe suffering will be greatly alleviated in this world as humans begin to understand their true nature of love, light and wisdom. We are committed to the realization of the true self in all beings, seeing that "Grace" is the wind that blows one in the direction of truth.

We invite you to become a member of Grace Foundation, in which you will receive our free bi-monthly newsletter, discounts on products from Grace Catalog and discounts on the many services we offer.

Some of which are:

Guided trips to the sacred sites of India and Bali

Retreats and seminars across the country

Reach out programs for troubled teens

Sacred Insights counseling and educational programs

Sacred Space Creations, providing free assistance to create a beautiful sacred space in your home or office.

Grace Catalog is an unlimited source of tools and inspirational gifts for conscious living. Please call for a free catalog 1-800-282-5292 or visit our web page at http:// www.gracefoundation.org or email at info@gracefoundation.org

About Jaya Sarada

Jaya has lived most of her life in Ojai, California, where she was deeply nurtured from the Theosophical Society since early childhood. Living just a short distance from the Oak Meadow where J. Krishnamurti spoke yearly, she attended these sacred talks throughout her life. Jaya has traveled to India, Switzerland and England to listen to Krishnamuriti's profound wisdom.

Her search for truth has lead her to India to live and participate in Ashrams where she deepened her realization of the sacred nature of life. Jaya has an MA in Transpersonal Psychology, and has been a therapist, healer and spiritual counselor for the past 20 years From the deep awareness of the suffering of life, her devotion to understanding the sacred nature of the self, and the cessation of suffering is her life long quest. In this devotion, there is only service for which she patiently awaits life's calling.

She now lives on Whidbey Island, Washington with her family, Tom and Arielle.

To reach Jaya Sarada by email, please write to:
JayaSarada@gracefoundation.org

Asatho maa sad gamaya
From the unreal, lead me to the real
Thamso maa jyothir gamaya
From darkness, lead me into the light
Mrthyor maa amrtham gamaya
From Death lead me into Immortality

Om Shanti, Om Shanti, Om Shanti